THEOLOGY IN ANGLICANISM

DAVID BATEMAN

The Anglican Studies Series

Theodore Alan McConnell
General Editor

What Is Anglicanism?
  Urban T. Holmes III

The Spirit of Anglicanism
  William J. Wolf, John E. Booty & Owen C. Thomas

Anglican Spirituality
  William J. Wolf, editor

The Anglican Moral Choice
  Paul Elmen, editor

Anglicanism and the Bible
  Frederick Houk Borsch, editor

Theology in Anglicanism
  Arthur A. Vogel, editor

Anglican Theology and Pastoral Care
  James E. Griffiss, editor

Theology in Anglicanism

Arthur A. Vogel, editor

Morehouse Barlow
Wilton

Morehouse Barlow Co., Inc.
78 Danbury Road
Wilton, Connecticut 06897

ISBN 0-8192-1344-6

Library of Congress Catalog Card Number 84-60624

Composition by The Publishing Nexus Incorporated
1200 Boston Post Road, Guilford, Connecticut 06437

Printed in the United States of America

Contents

Preface

When first conceived by the publisher, this volume was tentatively entitled, *Anglican Theology*. Approached to edit such a book, I declined, but I hastened to reply that I would be pleased to edit a volume entitled, *Theology in Anglicanism*.

The first title has a better ring to it, but the second one seems more accurate. Anglicans have always claimed to have no theology of their own, just the theology of the undivided Church. The Anglican Communion, taken as an entity comprised of the independent provinces around the world, is not a confessional Church.

Anglicans have written no creedal statement peculiar to them; their claim to Catholicity has largely rested on their claim to have no theology but that of the undivided Catholic Church. It is commonly admitted by historians of different traditions and persuasions that the establishment of the Church of England was a political rather than a religious action. Henry the Eighth did not intend to found a new Church, and he did not depart theologically, in any substantial manner, from the faith of the Roman Catholic Church of.his day. When the break of the Church of England with Rome officially occurred in the reign of Elizabeth I, Elizabeth remarked that the Church of England followed or invented no new way; instead it continued in the way of the primitive Catholic Church as expressed by the most ancient fathers.

Every Church has a theology, but is the Anglican claim true that it has no theology of its own? Even if the Anglican claim is true, the point has been made that Anglicanism at least has a methodology of its own—a way of living and doing theology.

That point is well taken, and the threefold appeal to Scripture, reason, and tradition—a characteristic appeal of Anglicanism—is evidence of the fact. Maintaining the proper balance and tension between the three facets of the Christian life has become a distinguishable trait of Anglicanism, at least by self-claim, and it lies at the root of another feature of the Anglican way, comprehensiveness.

When Anglicans try to maintain the proper balance between Scripture, reason, and tradition, they are not dealing with three absolutes, three ingredients that stand outside each other and are only externally related. The Anglican view is that the one Christian life is based on the three resources and that these sources penetrate each other. Each is found within the others. Scripture, for example, is not an entity complete in itself outside of which reason and tradition stand; reason and tradition are found within Scripture. That is why applying reason and tradition for the understanding of Scripture unlocks, rather than perverts, Scripture. Scripture is a permanent deposit of the living tradition of the early Church, as that tradition was reasonably discerned by the community of faith which produced the Scriptures. Similarly, reason is not extrinsic to Scripture and tradition; the latter informs reason, giving it data it would otherwise not have. Moreover, in the Christian view, human reasoning needs redemption as much as any other human activity. Tradition, to round out our considerations, cannot be itself apart from Scripture and reason. Within this tension of what has been called the threefold strands of the Anglican cord, Anglicans try to discern God's revelation of himself to his people.

Anglican comprehensiveness, when truly itself, results from the attempt to keep the tension between these three sources of Christian living open and dynamic, rather than allowing any one of them to become absolutized in such a manner that the other two are rendered useless or unimportant. If, as we maintain, each of these strands has the other two within its own fabric, to destroy any one of them is to destroy them all. That is a way of understanding what might be called "the problem of Anglicanism."

It is the purpose of this volume to offer a sample of *Theology in Anglicanism* as that theology is articulated and lived today. An historical context for the sample is presented in the first chapter; with that introduction, we turn to chapters which explicate major dimensions of the Christian life. After finishing *Theology in Anglicanism*, the reader may decide for his or her self whether or not the way Anglicans live and do theology has produced an Anglican Theology.

Arthur A. Vogel

1

The Context of Faith and Theology in Anglicanism

Henry Chadwick

To be a Christian is to be a member of Christ's Church. To believe in Christ is to believe in him in his Church—not apart from the Church, and to draw close to him is to draw close to all those who are his. To affirm "Jesus is Lord" is not only to make a basic statement of personal belief, it is also to share in the corporate confession of the whole Church.

The salient elements of this corporate confession can be simply described. Christians believe in:

1. God the Father, creator of all both seen and unseen, the source of power and goodness, beginning, middle, and end of all things, the God in whom we live and move and have our being;

2. The need of alienated, lost, but not irredeemable humanity for restoration, for reconciliation both to our Maker and to our brothers and sisters of our own and other races and tribes;

3. Jesus Christ, unique pattern and embodiment of what God our Creator intended humanity to be in love, self-giving, and obedience, without touch of self-concern; and at the same time, the life through and in which we see the very face of God, our Redeemer and so the mediator to his

people both of the forgiveness of sins and of eternal life—
gifts that almighty God alone may bestow;

4. The community of believers, incorporated into Christ by
faith and baptism, and continually renewed in their life in
the Spirit by participation together in the repeated memo-
rial thanksgiving or 'eucharist.' For Christ has not left his
people orphans: the common life of the community is a
gift of the Holy Spirit of God himself, teaching God's
people the way of holy discipline, making individual con-
sciences alive and alert to care for the needy (not only
within the Christian society, though there have always
been many poor folk there), to seek to uphold justice in
face of oppression, exploitation, and inhumanity; to foster
and strengthen peacefulness, honesty, truthfulness, and
goodness, wherever those often controversial and mar-
ginalized qualities may be found; to love mercy, and to
walk humbly with God; to do good to all men, and
especially to the household of God the Church;

5. The momentous significance of decisions in this life not
only for human peace and survival in a world that by pride
and greed we turn into a threat or actuality of battle,
murder, and sudden death, but also for our destiny
beyond this transitory life of suffering and unending
moral conflict; that is, Christians believe in the calling of
God to his people to share in the communion of saints and
the life everlasting, and in the transcendent significance of
moral choices in this life. Such belief enjoins Christians to
take seriously the language of heaven and hell.

This statement of belief is an affirmation characteristic of
Christian tradition, originating in the apostolic confession of
faith to which the Christian Scriptures bear witness and continuing in the tradition of the historical Christian community.
The node of divine revelation is discerned in the process of
redemption and reconciliation.

The early Church found itself engaged in debate with those
who interpreted the person of Christ as either merely so human
as to seem himself part of the world needing redemption, or so
exclusively divine as to lose solidarity with the human race.
Moreover, the triadic language of the New Testament about God
('Father, Son, and Holy Spirit' [Mt 28:19]; 'the grace...'
[2 Cor 13:14]) generated debate about the true understanding
of the doctrine of the Trinity—whether it should be interpreted

as a psychological analogy of an overriding and ultimate unity within which there is a plurality of aspects (e.g., knowing, remembering, loving) or as a social analogy of a shared life. There was also strong disagreement about human nature. If God's moral law is expressed in terms of positive and negative commands, and if man made in the image of God is endowed with an inalienable rationality, freedom, and capacity for deliberation, then it may be urged that man is responsible for moral choices, and destiny is not decided simply by the irresistible force of predestinating grace. On the other hand, such libertarian doctrines appear to encourage human moralistic pride and to deny the sovereignty of divine transcendence. The orthodox in their estimate of human nature sought a middle way between saying that man retains the capacity to solve his problems and saying that man is so corrupt as to be hopelessly irredeemable. The Christians all took it for granted that human nature as it now is falls far short of the Creator's intention, and is in will, though not in original nature, 'abnormal.' In short, the central Christian tradition affirms that man is not so good as to need no redemptive grace, nor so bad as to be unable to benefit from divine aid and the deep therapy of sacramental grace.

The answers to these questions were not obvious from a plain and simple reading of Holy Scripture. The continuing life of the Christian community makes constant reference to the writings of the apostolic Church and to the Old Testament Scriptures which it interprets in the light of Jesus Christ, the culmination of prophetic aspiration and the embodiment of God's new law and universal wisdom. But the New Testament is not a systematic and ordered treatise on theology. Its diversities are contained within a more fundamental unity—the focal point found in the person and work of Christ; but even within the apostolic Church itself there was powerful disagreement about the permissible limits of diversity. Charismatic gifts are good, taught St. Paul, but not if they divide the Church into factions censorious of one another. There is a higher knowledge and wisdom beyond simple faith, but it becomes inauthentic if and when those who are more advanced begin to despise their weaker brethren.

To maintain and protect the scattered Christian communities in eucharistic communion and in obedience to the word of God against gnostic theosophy, the second-century Church formed three principle instruments. They were, in the order of their appearance, the succession of ministerial episcopal order, the baptismal creed or confession of faith, and the canon of the New Testament Scriptures. Each was developed by an almost unselfconscious consensus as something essential to the Church's unity in the truth. We do not hear until a fairly late date of formal action by church councils, not even on the last point of the limits of the biblical canon.

The second-century Churches regarded the bishops of these communities as representatives, for the bishops embodied the apostolic tradition to a special degree. The apostolicity of the Church which, in line with the epistle to the Ephesians, is affirmed in the Catholic creeds, is not so total in its absorption as to obliterate a particular apostolicity of ministry, and there is no necessary tension between general and specific. All God's people receive by baptism a status that is a divine call and gift of grace. But not all within the community have the same role to perform. Though there is a priestly ministry belonging to the entire Church, not all baptized Christians receive the ministerial commission to shepherd the flock, to care for the word and sacraments, and to perform defined, specific acts in Christ's name for the service of his people. So the succession of ministerial order is never an end in itself, but a means to an end. It has no proper existence apart from the community it serves, and yet its authority is not derived by simple delegation from the community but is a gift of Christ to the community. So also if there is a priestliness to the ministry of the Church's pastors, that will not be derived by particularization from the universal priesthood the New Testament ascribes to the whole Church—because the Body of Christ participates in the high priestly intercession of the Head. It is a distinct gift of the grace of God to enable the ordained ministry to serve the Church in specific ways.

Within the New Testament itself (Ti 1:9) the function of a bishop is seen as safeguarding the Church from the bright ideas of private enterprise and as preserving the authentic sacred tradition. A bishop is to "teach what he has been taught." Then he will be "fit to rule" wisely over the Church of God

(1 Tm 3:1-7). This preservative and safeguarding role is exercised in fellowship by the collective society of bishops as representatives of their Churches.

A watershed in the development of the apostolic Church was marked by the great council at Jerusalem, described in Acts 15. The issue before that council was of the first magnitude: was the newborn community to remain a sect within a Judaism already accustomed to a wide diversity of sects (such as the community that gave us the Dead Sea Scrolls) or was it to be a world-wide universal body with both Jewish and non-Jewish members? A generation or two later the rapid spread of the Gentile mission made another such representative council harder to gather. We hear of no second-century council to combat Gnostic heresy. The fight was left to local bishops in their correspondence with each other. Before the end of the second century, however, councils of bishops did meet to decide on common policy toward the charismatic prophecy of the Montanists in Phrygia, to move toward agreement about the correct method of calculating the date of Easter, and to discuss other difficult questions.

A sentence in Tertullian (ca. 200) suggests that one of the topics discussed at these early councils was the limits of the New Testament canon. This was a matter on which the Christian Churches had (and have) not found it easy to reach full agreement. In Syria the Christian communities did not include in their New Testament the Revelation of St. John, 2 Peter, 2 and 3 John, and Jude. The status and authorship of the epistle to the Hebrews long remained a point of amicable debate. Gradually, the majority of Churches in both East and West accepted the canon of New Testament books common to the Orthodox Churches, Roman Catholics, Anglicans (Episcopalians), and Reformation Churches. The Syrian Jacobites retained (and retain to this day) the old Syrian canon, omitting the Revelation and other catholic epistles listed above. More controversial was the debate about the limits of the Old Testament. The Greek translation of the Old Testament, called the Septuagint or translation of the Seventy, made at Alexandria in the third century B.C., includes books such as Tobit, Judith, 1 and 2 Maccabees, the Wisdom of Solomon, the Wisdom of Ben-Sira

(Ecclesiasticus), and additions to the book of Daniel, which have no corresponding text in the old Hebrew canon. Although the Septuagint was the Bible frequently quoted by St. Paul and although it became the lectionary Bible of the Gentile Churches, it could not safely be appealed to in controversy with rabbis using only the Hebrew canon. The overplus of the Greek Old Testament was part of the Church's Bible, but could not be used in controversy to establish a doctrinal point, since in a controversy one cannot appeal to authority unless it is an authority recognized by all parties to the dispute. The books in this overplus therefore remained canonical, being read in the lectionary of Churches and cited as illustrative matter in sermons on ethical subjects, but not used in doctrinal debate. (Other than, perhaps, the creation out of nothing [2 Mc 7:28], there were and are no critical points of dogma dependent on the texts from these books.)

The Anglican Communion in the sixteenth century did not follow the radical Reformation demand (first formulated by Carlstadt, 1521) that the books in the Septuagint canon not included in the Hebrew text should be excluded from the lectionary. Luther included the books (except 1 and 2 Esdras) in his translation (1534) with a preface commending them; but the Reformed and Puritan traditions sought to distinguish between the certainly inspired books and, to them, equally certainly uninspired books of merely human authority, whose usage rested on ancient tradition. The negative estimate of the (misleadingly) so-called "Apocrypha" found expression in the Westminster Confession (1646–47). The Council of Trent in 1548 affirmed the books to be fully canónical. That the first generation of English Reformers did not dissent is shown by the large number of citations from the Apocrypha in the books of *Homilies* (1547 and 1571). At the revision of the English Prayer Book in 1661 a decision was deliberately made not to accede to the Puritan demand that the Apocrypha should be excluded from the lectionary.

Article 6 of the Thirty-nine Articles of 1571 declares Holy Scripture to be "those canonical books of the Old and New Testaments of whose authority was never any doubt in the Church." The clause implies a recognition of the force of church tradition and conciliar consensus in establishing canonicity, and, at the same time, concedes that disputed books have a less certain status. The intention may have been to try to contain within the comprehensive Elizabethan Church the Puritans who frowned at the Apocrypha, but the wording implies a questioning of the authenticity of Revelation, Hebrews, 2 Peter, etc. that perhaps the authors of the Article did not recognize.

The controversialists of the sixteenth century did not ask themselves historical questions about the way in which the Church acquired a biblical canon. They did not question the function of the Old Testament within the life of the first Churches, nor did they question the interpretation of the Old Testament as "prophecy" fulfilled in the Gospel, with Christ vindicating the claims of Scripture and Scripture vindicating him as the realization of God's promises. It followed that the oral proclamation of Christ's message came to the first Christians with a "Thus saith the Lord" parallel to that of the Old Testament, and then that Christ's commissioned apostles exercised an interpretative ministry which, eventually, their successors sought to save or to recover by preserving whatever could be found of their writings. The preserved writings point to the centers of authority: the martyred apostles Peter and Paul (Acts, Pauline epistles, St. Mark's Gospel, then the Petrine epistles), James and Jude (the holy family tradition), John (the Ephesian tradition), the Apocalypse of John (Patmos). Apostolicity became for the second-century Churches a criterion of authentic Christianity. Since prophets were by definition inspired, it was the most natural thing in the world for the apostles to be treated as no less inspired, and, therefore, for apostolic writings to be treated as reverentially as the Old Testament prophets. So it came about that the concept of apostolic succession, applied to the problem of ministerial order before the end of the first century (Clement of Rome), was formulated half a century or more later in terms of the apostolic writings (Irenaeus). Continuity in the Apostles' teaching and fellowship, in sacramental life, and in corporate worship (Acts 2:42) as the sign of the Spirit guiding the people of God in all truth was preserved through the storms of the second-century conflicts by the episcopal office and by the collection of apostolic writings.

To affirm the foundational importance of the canon of the New Testament is to imply that these writings constitute a norm or criterion of authentic witness to Christ and his meaning for the people of God. The Church is prior to the Scriptures, which constitute the earliest written Christian testimony. It is relatively unimportant whether or not particular books come directly from the apostolic authors to whom they are attributed, for the question of canonicity cannot be a purely historical question. Canonicity is a judgment by the Christian community acknowledging certain writings to be its normative record of foundation. But the Holy Spirit who has given the Church these writings is also the Spirit present and active in the community in all generations.

The sixteenth century was not the earliest century to work with an antithesis of written against unwritten tradition, but the contrast between the original sources and the decayed forms of late medieval Christian practice encouraged people of that age to draw an equally sharp contrast between the Bible and the community. When Martin Luther's onslaught on the sale of indulgences was met by appeals to the authority of the Pope and the tradition of the medieval Church, it was natural that he should reply by taking his stand on Scripture as higher authority. The left wing of the Reformation declined to acknowledge that the Church had any authority, insisting on the authority of "Scripture alone." It was a vulnerable position, for (1) the principle "Scripture alone" cannot be read out of Scripture alone (an objection which is more than a debating point); (2) this principle may easily be taken to mean (or rather, some ingenuity has to be deployed to show that it does not mean) that nothing is essential to salvation that is not perfectly self-evident to any and every casual reader of the Bible; (3) appeal to Scripture alone presupposes that the meaning of Scripture is so clear on all material points that everyone will be in agreement. In practice nothing resembling agreement appears; the Reformation, for example, emerged as a large group of fissiparous groups and sects; (4) it is hard to state the principle of "Scripture alone" and do justice to the role of the Church in the recognition and canonizing of the biblical books; (5) most groups in the Reformation, especially Calvinists, held strongly to the tradition of a Sunday Sabbath. All attempts to argue that the assimilation of the Christian Sunday to the Jewish Sabbath is an evident deduction from Holy Scripture suffer from special pleading; they tend to convince only those already predisposed to the conclusion on other grounds.

On the other hand, there was also weakness in the conservative defenses in the Reformation. The learned scholars of the Renaissance had created an atmosphere of critical doubt toward received opinions. Dionysius the Areopagite, the Isidorian papal decretals, the Donation of Constantine, and even some traditional parts of the New Testament text (the ending of St. Mark's Gospel, the heavenly witnesses of 1 John 5:8, the angel of the agony in Luke 22, the woman taken in adultery in John 8), were being treated as inauthentic. The scholarly spirit contrasted the present with the sources and sought authenticity in unencrusted originals. Moreover, while there seemed much force in the contention that the Church has authority as interpreter of the Bible, it was a weakness that so much in the library of ecclesiastical interpretation consisted of allegory. A gradually mounting volume of exegesis in late medieval times had tended to treat historical exegesis as primary and distinct from more spiritual interpretation, not (as Origen had thought in the third century) almost marginal and accidental to the divine intention. When some reformers went so far as to reject all allegory and to insist that the authentic sense could be discovered by purely scholarly exegesis and by study of the ancient original languages, they continued a process that would inevitably end in painful tension between historical theology and dogmatics. To some, the Bible appeared almost irrelevant to religion.

Among the problems faced by the conservative defense in the sixteenth century, one must reckon the unlimited charcter of the appeal to "tradition." Almost any position could be made impregnable if the defender had to show only that the practice had been going on for some time; e.g., communion in only one kind (from the ninth century) or pardoners selling indulgences (gradual growth after the Crusades). The best conservative defenders conceded abuses. Their diffiuclty was to make a clear distinction between kernel and husk. Where did the one end and the other begin? The sixteenth-century debate was bedeviled by the axiom, common to both Catholic and Protestant, that historical change is synonymous with corruption, that whatever is authentic in Christian tradition is unaltered and unalterable, that whatever can be shown to be a late development in church history must be an adulteration of primary, immutable truth. The distinction between mutable and immutable became fused with the distinction between tradition and Scripture, the former being adapted by ecclesiasitcal decision makers according to the circumstances of the age or the place. The Council of Trent's long debate on Scripture and tradition ended by stressing that the saving truth of the Gospel is not confined to the written documents of the Bible—and by censuring those that despised tradition, e.g., the list of canonical books accepted in the Church, or Jerome's "vulgate" translation as the authoritative Latin version used in western Churches. At the same time those traditions that are to be held with a respect equal to that accorded Scripture are limited to faith and morals; they do not include matters of ceremonial practice. It was axiomatic for Trent both that the Church cannot define anything not consonant with Scripture and that the Spirit who inspired Scripture also safeguards their authentic interpretation through the Church's proper, authoritative organs of teaching. Radical Protestants attacked these axiomatic propositions as being mutually inconsistent, which was not necessarily so.

The Anglicans saw the problem as one of the Church's continuity. To reform the Church by freeing it of abuses is not to make a new Church. Richard Hooker "gladly acknowledged" the Roman Church to be "of the family of Jesus Christ," while reserving his position on certain points. For the Anglicans the main stumbling block was the originating cause of the English Reformation, namely, the desire to be free of Roman jurisdiction, of curial interference with ecclesiastical appointments, and of high fees for legal services, which were in any event resented. Adherents to the mainstream of Anglican theology did not readily accuse the papacy of having become Antichrist, though some exegetes of the more esoteric parts of the book of Daniel and of St. John's Apocalypse were sure that this must be so, feeling consternation when they read moderate Protestants such as Grotius (1583–1645), who expounded these texts very differently. In England Joseph Mede (or Mead) (1586–1638) astonished his readers by combining a conviction that the Roman Church authentically taught the fundamental doctrines of the faith and indeed preserved the sacrificial character of the Eucharist more effectively and more scripturally than the Church of England, with an elaborate interpretation of the Apocalypse that put the papacy in an unhappy light. The occult and cabbalistic interests of some of the seventeenth-century Cambridge Platonists, especially Henry More (1614–87), led to fearful pictures of papal corruption portrayed in colors all the harsher and more lurid because directed less against distant Roman Catholics than against immediate neighbors, namely, brother Anglicans who adopted an altogether milder assessment of the mistakes of the Latin Church and were disinclined to see even in the ineptitudes of James II the very wiles of the Man of Sin. One cannot read Henry More without noticing how uncharacteristic he is of Anglican theology of the seventeenth century, and how relatively small his influence was to be on the future shape of English theology. But his books, especially *A Modest Enquiry into the Mystery of Iniquity* (1644), take the cover off a malodorous and implacable popular hatred of Catholic faith and practice that would have appalled Richard Hooker, John Bramhall, or Herbert Thorndike.

There remained an intractable and recalcitrant element in the Anglican tradition that militated for the continuity and acknowledged visibility of the Church; for instance, great care had been taken on 17 December 1559 to ensure preservation of apostolic succession when Matthew Parker was consecrated Archbishop of Canterbury by *four* bishops— though many of those who had been bishops under the Catholic Queen Mary had refused cooperation and it was one of those close-run things that from time to time enliven the pages of church history. (In 556, a pope whose appointment was controversial could find only two instead of the canonically required three to consecrate him, and the third consecrator had to be a presbyter.) The decision, in defiance of the Genevan party on the Calvinist side, to maintain the episcopal order continued to be upheld even through periods when the Puritan tide was rising high, until finally the storm broke over the heads of Archbishop William

Laud and King Charles I. The sixteenth-century Anglicans had to be content to argue against the Calvinist view that the presbyterian system is that of the apostolic age and that it is, therefore, prescribed by "divine right." Richard Hooker's *Laws of Ecclesiastical Polity* initially contends that no single form of church government is of divine right but that the Church has power so to order the pastoral ministry that episcopacy is entirely proper and legitimate, a view profoundly unacceptable to the Calvinists in Scotland, by whom episcopacy was spewed out as a usurpation contrary to God's will for his true Church, its presence deemed a mark of the Antichrist. Hooker's seventh book more boldly advanced the view that the original institution of bishops in succession to the apostles was of God: "...the Holy Ghost was the author it it" (vii,5,10).

The English Ordinal presupposed that the threefold order of bishop, presbyter, and deacon is a sign and instrument of unity and continuity in the Church, and that while both bishops and presbyters share in the common responsibilities attaching to priesthood (namely, presiding at the Eucharist and pronouncing absolution to the penitent), the bishop is distinct from the presbyter in being the minister of ordination and confirmation. Because of the bishop's general responsibility for his diocese, he is understood to have "jurisdiction," that is, the ultimate power to put an end to scandal by requiring compliance or withdrawal. Hooker, like Clement of Rome at the end of the first century, sees the duly ordained ministry as embodying the principle that God wills order in his Church, and that by this ordered life there is no constriction of spiritual gifts. Ecclesiastical authority and spiritual power are distinct, yet have a wide overlap with one another. For both office and charism have no role apart from the entire society of the whole Church of God, and the office of ministry bestowed from God through the medium of ordination is one to which there is attached a spiritual gift. St. Paul exhorts Timothy to stir up the gift of the Spirit given through the laying on of hands (2 Tm 1:6), and such language presupposes a sacramental understanding of the nature of ordination with outward sign and inward gift within the Church, which is the very body of Christ.

Division and suspension of eucharistic communion have

generated painful problems about the status of ministry and sacraments in separated bodies. The Donatist schism in fourth-century North Africa provoked intense feeling between the divided bodies, with the usual symptoms of mutual suspicion, prickliness over mixed marriages, and absolute refusal by the Donatists to recognize validity in Catholic sacraments. St. Augustine of Hippo was moved to find reasons for dissenting from the general view of the ancient Church that there can be no authenticity outside the communion of the one universal Church grounded upon the apostolic foundation. In the third century, Pope Stephen had already argued against St. Cyprian of Carthage that valid baptism may be received outside that communion when it is duly given as Christ comanded and with orthodox faith. Augustine sought to extend this priniciple to the recognition of orders, but his argument was the subject of contemporary and subsequent dispute. His generous intention was to make reconciliation with the schismatics easier by allowing the unconditional validity of their ministerial order. One warms to the ecumenical intention behind Augustine's proposal, but one has to grant that his critics also had a point: the Augustinian argument seemed to weaken the axiom that the ordained ministry can have no proper existence apart from the community of the Spirit in which that ministry is called to exercise its function and office. Augustine's argument seemed to encourage people to think that ordination by a bishop in apostolic succession might be the source and criterion of ecclesial validity, *taken by itself.* The Church before Augustine's time did not think in that way. When the Council of Nicaea (325) decreed that a bishop must be consecrated by the metropolitan with, if possible, all the bishops of the province or, if not all, a minimum of three, the Council understood that minimum of three bishops to be representative of the wider fellowship. The bishops present at the first ecumenical council would not have thought a person consecrated by any three bishops in any circumstances whatever and in defiance of all canonical procedure a claimant to catholic recognition. Such consecration lay close to the heart of what the early Church understood by "schism," an expression the opposite of charity. To love a community is not to be indifferent to it, not to act as if it hardly existed, certainly never to act in malicious rivalry to it.

It is a fact worth pondering that the early Christian communities under their bishops did not think of themselves as independent bodies, each following its own light, doing its own thing; rather, they thought of themselves as a realization in a particular place of the universal body of Christ and, therefore, not free to do anything they might wish in disregard of other Christians. That is not to say there was not a wide diversity of custom, especially liturgical custom. In fact, from time to time liturgical diversity caused both puzzlement and distress. In the middle of the fifth century A.D. Socrates, a lawyer at Constantinople and historian of the Church from the time of Constantine to his own day, remarked that differences of custom concerning the date of Easter had been the natural result of the fact that the apostles gave no direction in the matter, having more important things to do than to legislate annual festivals. "Those who agree in faith differ on questions of usage." He cited divergent customs in different regions regarding fasts, special services on Wednesdays and Fridays, and the marriage of clergy. More serious differences arose in the interpretation of the eucharistic liturgy: in the Greek East the climax of the consecration lay (as it still lies) in the invocation of the Holy Spirit, whereas in the Latin West, as one may see in Ambrose (bishop of Milan, 374–97), the climax is placed in the recitation by the presiding celebrant, acting in Christ's name, of the Lord's words at the last Supper. But the gradual growth of different interpretations and customs led to mutual unease only when East and West had other reasons for being edgy and dissatisfied with one another. Rome's claims to a universal jurisdiction over all Churches, including the older Churches of the East, never found a manner of expression that the East could accept; rather, it stimulated countercharges that when the western Churches altered the ecumenical creed to say that the Holy Spirit proceeded from the Father *and the son*, they had disqualified themselves from claiming that at Rome there was a guardian of the true and unchanging faith.

The Orthodox Churches of the East (in Greece, Russia, the Balkans, and now also widely spread in the West) have had difficulty dealing with the Roman Catholic beliefs that the bishop of Rome enjoys unique privileges among the successors of the apostles and that he is supreme among his brother bishops. That the bishop of Rome presides over the most ancient see, the very church where the apostles Peter and Paul taught and where they died as martyrs; that the bishop of Rome is patriarch with supraprovincial authority over the Latin West; that his see is or should be the bond and focus of unity in the eucharistic communion of all local Churches—all this may be accepted and affirmed. And there is no special difficulty about the proposition that in certain special circumstances, as when a ruling is needed on matters of either faith or morals cardinal to Christian belief or practice, the primate who is the focus of unity and continuity in the universal Church on earth can articulate the decision that a world-wide or ecumenical council would take. That is, there is no particular difficulty about the Roman Catholic doctrine of "papal infallibility," if it means that the bishop of Rome, in certain circumstances, becomes the organ or mouthpiece through which the implicit consensus of the faithful finds expression. There is a mountainous difficulty if it is being claimed that the pope is the source and criterion by which the Church—without him all too prone to error—is maintained in the truth, and that his pronouncement is the one necessary and sufficient condition for a reliable and final definition in resolution of a controversy. The mountainous difficulty assumes Himalayan proportions if it is urged that the first Vatican Council (1870) made a conciliar decision that the ex cathedra or very solemn definitions of the pope on faith and morals are irreformable in their own right, irrespective of any opinion the bishops may hold individually or collectively, and if it is also urged that without the pope such a council may well fall into error. One is stopped cold if a council is nothing without the pope but the pope never needs a council at all, for one is then faced with the awkward dilemma of having a definition of papal infallibility made by the first Vatican Council, and therefore a pope apparently in need of a council to agree that he did not need it.

The underlying problem here is only in part the consequence of the general imprecision of Roman Catholic theory about papal authority. It is also linked to the question of conciliar authority. The Anglican tradition has been strongly stamped with conciliar modes of thinking; that is to say, the synodical gathering of bishops representing their local dioceses derives its authority from the body or bodies that have a stake in its deliberations and decisions. The wisdom of many is in general better than that of one, but only the assistance of the Holy Spirit can make a council, or any other human agency, secure against error. Early Christian councils met with the presence of Christ symbolized by the open Gospel and with the prayerful confidence that the Spirit would surely lead his Church into truth in those many matters where Scripture gave no guidance. The Lord had promised his presence when two or three were gathered in his name. The ancient Church did not understand this to mean that two or three bishops could be infallible. The moral unanimity of a council of many bishops has always been understood to have decision-making and binding force for the community represented. The Spirit gives the spiritual gift of discernment and spiritual judgment to baptized believers, as well as to the commissioned teachers of the Church. The consensus of bishops in council is therefore integrally linked to the wider, universal consensus of all the faithful, both clerical and lay; and that wider consensus has often exercised, gradually but decisively, a controlling critical interpretation of the decrees and definitions of even general councils. The reception of the believing community is integral to the process of authoritative doctrinal or ethical decisions. In this process of reception the assent of major Christian leaders, patriarchs and metropolitans, and the pope himself, is an evident and practical necessity. The binding force of a definition is determined, however, not by a single bishop but by the agreement of all the bishops representing the universal Church.

The charism of discernment given to all baptized believers is another way of speaking of the priesthood, which by analogy to and derivation from the unique high priesthood of Christ himself, inheres in the whole Church according to New Testament teaching. The doctrine of the priesthood of all believers is misinterpreted if it is taken to mean that clergy are really only a special sort of laymen, identified by unusual clothing, differentiated from the laity merely by some aptitude for running clubs for the young and by training in the dramatic art of staging that impressive visual aid, a sacramental celebration. This is not how Anglicans understand the ministry and sacraments. To be a priest is to share in the calling to be a commissioned representative of God, bringing God to humanity and humanity to God and serving as a channel of communication between the holy and the unholy. It is a sacrificial and intercessory calling. The quintessence of Christian priesthood does not lie in the performance of quasi-Levitical functions, but in the transformation of human existence in a community through the opening up of man to the action of the Spirit and to the divine gift of love.

From time to time in Christian history the freedom of the individual to be himself or herself and to pursue the truth is felt to be in tension with the custom of the community. The individual's thinking may appear to challenge conservative minds, which fear that freedom is being used to disrupt the coherence of the society, perhaps even to endanger the very lifeline of salvation in the Christian Gospel. The duty of authority often is not to bring discussion and debate to a speedy end by promptly taking one side or the other, but rather to see that at the end of the affair legitimate options are kept open. Men of reason, men of equal devotion and love for God and his Church, may disagree on weighty matters. One has only to think of the impassioned debate about whether or not peace can be maintained in this world without threat of retaliation. It is normally a mark of men of reason that they are aware and can see the inherent force of the arguments deployed by those with whom they deeply disagree. Sometimes a religious thinker may feel in conscience bound to adopt a position that not only offends official authority but that seems blatantly mistaken to good men and women who love God but have not seen matters with the same eyes. The tradition of Christian doctrine is, like Holy Scripture in a famous image of Pope Gregory the Great, a river in which lambs may paddle and elephants swim. The independent thinker exploring fresh ways of interpreting the faith is not without human frailties; he may have in him an itch to astonish or even the illusion that the only way to rouse torpid minds from indolent convention is to subject them to rude shocks purposely calculated to enrage. A clear view of the proper proportion of things is normally achieved only by the most strenuous mental effort. Nevertheless, in the long run, the process of reception by the faithful is as critical in significance for the individual theologian as it is for the decisions of the teaching authority of the Church through conciliar or primatial definition. The Church, whose history offers many examples of its genius for transforming *enfants terribles* into elder statesmen, is also a body which has had much to learn from men, such as Jeremiah, Athansius, or Martin Luther, who did not always say what everybody wanted to hear.

It is certain, and in the Christian tradition quite non-controversial, that the individual must above all things follow conscience—conscience informed and illuminated with the best light available, not simply the irrational "jack-in-the-box" of a hunch that some twentieth-century writers have mistaken for the moral sense and judgment (as if all human beings know of right and wrong were imbibed with mother's milk, quite divorced from social need and careful deliberation). But the individual Christian also knows that it is a short step from the inner light to the outer darkness, and that there are always subtle and not-so-subtle temptations to vanity and self-assertion.

The Anglican/Episcopalian tradition has found authority in a balance of things: in Holy Scripture, in the interpretative shared faith of the community that we call "tradition," the individual's informed reason and conscience, the living voice of the Church through synodical or primatial decision (where the primate is articulating what a synod would say, as it were by anticipation), and, perhaps above all other sources and criteria, in the liturgies of the Prayer Book. The Prayer Book has been, without rival, the focus of Anglican doctrine and spirituality. Anglicans have never thought of Thomas Cranmer as the author of a systematic theology retaining normative value for succeeding generations, and indeed his writings are, with sufficient reason, familiar only to a handful of historians. There has been no time in Anglican history when a controversy could be settled by some apt quotation from Cranmer's works. In fact, Cranmer's personal theological position often appears at variance with the liturgies into which his genius was poured, for, as he went on, he was influenced in a Swiss or Zwinglian direction that never became characteristic of the mainstream of Anglican eucharistic piety.

Within the sixteenth-century Anglican Church there were

tensions between conservatives, tenacious of the Real Presence of Christ in the Eucharist and hostile to those who wanted to reduce the Eucharist to a love-feast between brethren, and the more radical protestants who branded the papacy as Antichrist and used the fear of "the scarlet woman of Babylon" to distance the Church of England from the emerging dogmatic decisions of the Council of Trent. The occasional inconsistencies and ambiguities of the Thirty-nine Articles may be attributed to lack of success in reconciling these tensions. In the religious turmoil of the sixteenth century, the Church of England felt the need for doctrinal statement. Under Henry VIII this first was done by the Ten Articles of 1536, the Bishops' Book of 1537, the Six Articles of 1539, and the King's Book of 1543. In 1553, under Edward VI, Forty-three Articles were prepared, and these were revised (by the removal of some aggressively protestant elements) to produce the first edition of the Thirty-nine Articles in 1563—but not formally approved at that stage. Queen Elizabeth I had been sharply and abrasively snubbed by the pope early in her reign, being denounced as illegitimate and no lawful possessor of the Crown. She could not retain her independence of the superior political and military power of France and Spain if she identified her kingdom with the Catholic cause. Finally, in 1570, Pope Pius V issued the bull *Regnans in excelsis* declaring Elizabeth a usurper and heretic, relieving her subjects of their allegiance, and instructing them to disobey her laws. The consequential approval of the Thirty-nine Articles in 1571 identified the Crown and the Church of England with the denial that the bishop of Rome had any jurisdiction in England. Doctrinally, the Articles were more protestant in rhetoric than in substance, and assent to them was required of the clergy; they were not printed with the Prayer Book until early in the eighteenth century, and it was exceptional for English laity not at the universities to know much about them.

The status of the Articles in Anglican theology has long been unclear. Their structure is loose, and it is evident that they cannot provide—and cannot have been intended to provide—an adequate rule of faith. Several expressions in them are intelligible only to those who have some familiarity with the writings of the medieval schoolmen. They are unsatisfactory to Calvinists, for they do not teach the five essential Calvinist propositions of unconditional election, limited atonement, total depravity of man, irresistible grace, and the final perseverence of the saints in indefectible grace. (The last point is incompatible with Article 16.) Because the Articles teach justification by grace and by faith alone, but say nothing of justification resting on the imputation of Christ's merits and not on an inherent or imparted righteousness as the Holy Spirit molds the character of the believing soul, they are insufficient to strict Lutherans. Article 28 teaches, regarding the Eucharist, that "the Body of Christ is given, taken, and eaten in the Supper, only after an heavenly and spiritual manner," that it is not a mere sign of the love that Christians ought to have among themselves but a sacrament of our redemption, and that "to such as rightly, worthily, and with faith receive the same, the Bread which we break is a partaking of the Body of Christ; and likewise the Cup of Blessing is a partaking of the Blood of Christ." This highly traditional language is juxtaposed with a critique of the notion that the presence of Christ in the sacred elements is by the annihilation (or cessation) of the metaphysical substance of the bread and wine (transubstantiation)—the very possibility of which would become meaningless after the seventeenth-century scientists and philosophers had challenged the Aristotelian domination of the schools; but even within an Aristotelian metaphysic of substance, the language is beset with logical conundrums. Yet Article 28 uses terms ("The Body of Christ is given, taken, and eaten . . . ") emphatically affirming the objective presence of Christ, i.e., the consecrated bread is Christ's Body before it is taken into the hand and eaten, but the reception belongs wholly to the order of grace, not of nature. Faith is the condition of worthy reception, but the Article does not make subjective faith the distinguishing mark for deciding whether or not the Body of Christ is present. It is, perhaps, specially significant that the one point in the Articles where anathema occurs is in Article 18, with the laying of a solemn curse on the ultraliberal opinion that the mediation of salvation through Christ is a matter of indifference, and that "every man shall be saved by the law or sect which he professes" provided his conduct follows natural law.

The Thirty-nine Articles have had some influence in the formation of the Anglican middle way between Rome and Protestantism, but they have never enjoyed the standing of binding rules of faith. Three of the most learned and eminent archbishops of the seventeenth century, William Laud (1573–1645), James Ussher (1581–1656), and John Bramhall (1594–1663), held that the clergy were not bound by their assent to agree at every point, but only not to attack publicly the Articles. The requirement for any assent at all was criticized as tyrannizing the conscience by seventeenth-century Calvinists and by liberal Latitudinarians in the eighteenth century and after. In some parts of the Anglican Communion today the Articles enjoy no standing, while in others they are printed (often with the Prayer Book), but without assent being required. In the provinces of Canterbury and York they are treated as a historical witness, which has played a part in the formation of the characteristically Anglican mind, but the form of assent does not now presuppose more than that.

Gilbert Burnet (1699) expounded the Thirty-nine Articles as an expression of "comprehensiveness," saying this should not suggest a compromise with truth in which concessions of principle are made, nor a syncretism of incompatibilities, but a deliberate choice by authority not to close off legitimate opinions within the broad and deep tradition of catholic spirituality and faith.

2

Reason, Faith, and Mystery

Arthur A. Vogel

We would do well to begin our considerations with a definition of religion, and we may use as our definition that religion is *the recognition of and the responsive life-relationship with the ultimate reality of the universe*. People do not consciously have to use that definition in their religious lives, but there is reason to believe that their religion, if it is held up for examination, will be found to have the features we have suggested. Religion must certainly be involved with reality, and only ultimate reality—or what appears to be ultimate reality—can adequately account for the total claim religion characteristically makes on a person's life.

Christians hold that the ultimate reality of the universe is not *in* the universe; such reality is beyond the universe in the sense of being different from it. Not distant, just different.

Ultimate reality demands a life-response, that is to say, a response from which no portion of one's life is omitted, for no aspect of a person's life can be unaffected by ultimate reality. But of primary importance for us at the moment is the fact that religion always involves the polarity of, and the tension between, recognition and response. There is no such thing as a religion of pure cognition or a religion of pure response, although in the ongoing lives of people and communities one pole or the other tends to predominate. Some people try to make a religion of "doing," while others try to make a religion of "the book."

There is also a tension between the reality of this world and the reality of God who is different from the world. How different can God be? If he is not different enough, he cannot be God, and if he is too different, he cannot be known—he disappears or is not able to appear. Our discussion in this chapter will take place within these tensions, so Anglicans, with their penchant for tension, should feel at home.

There is still another tension within our religious lives, however, to which we must pay special attention. This tension has assumed special importance in our day and is the one we must look at first if we hope to do justice to the special nature of Christianity. It is the tension between history and abstract thought.

The problem arises when we consider whether or not Christianity is reasonable. What is the relation of reason to religion? What is the nature of faith? How can we talk about God if God is different from the world? Throughout their distinguishable history, Anglicans have overwhelmingly opted for Christianity's reasonableness and the exercise of reason in religion. Their tradition has never embodied anti-intellectualism; still, they have never maintained that the truth of Christianity can be demonstrated. If it could, people could be intellectually forced to believe, and religion could be taught like mathematics.

It has been said that the historical nature of being is becoming more clearly understood in this century than in any previous period of human thought. The "simple idea of history" is being taken seriously in a new way, urged on by both the social and physical sciences. Human beings for the first time, we are told, are being understood in their "essential historicity." In such an understanding, a human being is recognized for the person he or she actually is only when he or she is accepted in the full, fleshly existence of his or her bodily life. Moeover, the concrete existence and givenness, not just of ourselvs, but of the whole universe which exists independently of us, is a feature of reality we must accept. We, and our thought, do not control everything, although we may examine everything coming to our attention by our thought.

Reason always begins its work with elements provided for it. Some of these elements may be supplied by history, and it is such historical givens which are especially important for Christianity. A religion that claims to be revealed, as Christianity does, obviously acknowledges the primacy of God and his independence of human reason. God exists in himself and does what he does for his own reasons. Christians, we have indicated, believe in a God who is different from the world; his difference is the way he is distinguished from the world, and it is the basis for saying that he is "above" the world. Because of God's difference, he is supernatural. He is above nature and for that reason above the unaided power of human reason to know him, for he lives in himself. The Prologue of the Gospel according to John makes the point when it says, "No one has ever seen God" (1:18). If any intimate knowledge of such a God is to be possible, God himself must be the source of it; a supernatural God, in other words, must reveal himself to human beings if he is to be known by them. Such a revelation is exactly what Christians believe has happened to people specially chosen for that purpose.

Revelation plays a unique role in Christianity, and the special claims of Christianity among the religions of the world depend upon the special nature of its revelation. Christianity is totally dependent upon certain contingent, historical events in its claim to be a revealed religion; if God did not enter history and speak through specific historic events and persons as Christians claim, there is no truth to Christianity. Nothing provably true about Christianity remains if the first Christian witnesses lied or if what they thought once happened did not happen. Christianity's absolute claims are based on events that may or may not have happened.

The total dependence of Christianity upon the revelation it believes comes from God underscores three important features of Christian faith: that God always takes the initiative; that God is personal; and that God is always concerned for persons in community.

God's difference from the world will be a continuing theme throughout this chapter, as it must be a continuing theme throughout the lives of believers. The acknowledgment of God's difference from us is the reason for Christianity's radical dependence on history for its knowledge of God. God is too different from us to be known in a positive way by our natural abilities alone, so God must decide where and how to reveal himself; in Christianity, the primacy of something given by God over which we have no control is inseparably linked with the uniqueness of certain historic events. There is no more convincing way for God to reveal to us that he is somehow personal than to reveal himself in history, for in human experience a person is fully himself only in his historic acts. Thus it has been said that the only way God could reveal himself as a Person to human beings was to give himself a history in the world. Christians believe he did that in Jesus.

Since the God of Christians is personal, the revelation of his nature is an encounter with a Person. Even in our human interrelations, although we can know a good deal about each other from independent external observation, our intimate knowledge of another person depends upon that person's willingness freely to reveal himself or herself to us. That must be even more the case if the Person we know is as different from us as God is.

Revelation, for a Christian, is the means of God's self-disclosure; it is nothing less than his presence in our lives, and that presence can never be grasped by—or reduced to—separate truths which can be stated in propositions and listed in books. If revelation is truly of God, it must reveal God for who and what he is in himself. No finite mind can ever know God as God knows himself; therefore, even in the intimacy of revelation, God remains a mystery to us.

The last remark should not be taken to mean that we are able to know no more about God after revelation than before; rather, it should be taken to mean that revelation does not reduce God to anything less than he is. The point we are trying to make can be illustrated from Scripture. Christian faith claims that Jesus Christ is the unique, final, and full revelation of God in human terms. The Epistle to the Colossians says that "in him the whole fullness of deity dwells bodily" (2:9). God in human life and human life in God are, for St. Paul, completely revealed in Jesus. God's final and lasting revelation in Jesus is also indicated in the Letter of Jude where believers are exhorted to "contend for the faith which was once for all delivered unto the saints" (1:3). But the finality of which the Epistle speaks is not a propositional or conceptual one, for as Paul puts it earlier in the Epistle previously quoted, Jesus is "the image of the invisible God" (Col 1:15). Jesus is an "image" of God and a "bodily" fullness of deity; he is, as we would say, a concrete, inexhaustible person, a moving image in time, with whom we can continue to live in time, not an abstract proposition about God which exists in an abstract world of ideas outside of time.

We may now look at the manner in which God's revelation is communal, but first we must say something about the role of individuals in it. Revelation separates people from each other and makes them dependent upon certain individuals who seem chosen for their task—for revelation is a gift from one person to another. This fact highlights a difference between religion and the experimental sciences.

Any worthwhile scientific formula derives its authority from experiments that verify it: an essential thing about the experiment is its repeatability, its independence from the first person who performed it, or, for that matter, from any particular person. Regarding what happens in a laboratory, the product, not the person, is the important thing. But as believers attempt to verify matters of faith in their daily lives, the case is quite the contrary; they are not freed from dependence upon the accepted authority of certain persons—saints, apostles, prophets, and teachers—who lived before them. St. Paul has played a unique role in describing the normative experience of God in Christ, for example, and the experience of Christians after St. Paul has not negated Paul's importance; if anything, later experience has intensified Paul's singular role and the dependence of others upon him. Why is that the case?

Scientific experimentation abstracts from the singularity of persons as completely as possible and judges in terms of impersonal measurability alone. Repeatability by anyone is the essence of a good scientific experiment; the goal of such an experiment is to render the experimenter anonymous. Religion, on the other hand, does not seek to negate personal differences; religion is a relationship between persons, and revelation, we have seen, is a gift from one person to another. A gift differentiates people and heightens personal identity rather than destroying it by rendering a person anonymous. So it is with revelation. Paul's experience of God has become a norm for the Christian experience of God; subsequent experience does not render Paul's experience unimportant, for it is only by means of Paul's experience that the community of faith judges subsequent experience to be Christian.[1]

Having looked at the special role of individuals in revelation, we must now go on to stress that, although the revelation of God in Christ is given to individuals, it is never given for individuals alone. It is given through individuals to a people, to a community, the community of faith. According to Christian belief, it was God's purpose in history to call a faithful people into existence, and it was the communal life and relationship with God of a special people that furnished the context and expectation which enabled the first believers to recognize Jesus as the Messiah, the Christ. Echoing God's call to Abraham (mentioned in Genesis) and God's words to Moses (recorded in Exodus), Christians are reminded that they are "a chosen race, a royal priesthood, a holy nation, God's own people . . . once you were no people but now you are God's people" (1 Pt 2:9f).

God chose himself a people, and individuals are saved by becoming members of that people. The faith of the community forms its members, and when the faith of both the old and new people of God was preserved in writing, the accepted books, the canon of Scripture of the Old and New Testaments, was determined by the community that used the books rather than by the authors who wrote them. As a matter of fact, many of the authors were unknown. The cooperativeness of reason, Scripture, and tradition did not lie dormant until it was emphasized by seventeenth-century Anglican divines; such roots penetrate to the very sources of our Judeo-Christian life. That is why appeal must be made to them.

In the early Church described in the Acts of the Apostles, "believers" was a way of referring to the community of people as a whole who accepted Jesus as the Messiah. We have spoken of the "community of faith." When a person believes in Jesus, that faith identifies him or her not only with Jesus but with the community which has become identified with Christ as his mystical body.

Once the Spirit of Christ was believed to have been given to the Church, it became impossible for anyone to think that Jesus could be separated or met in isolation from the community that believed in him. Actually, it was the faith of a community about Jesus to which an individual was called when he or she accepted the call to be a follower of Christ.

But what is faith? Although communities may express their faith, individuals join such communities by an act of faith, which is their own. What is the nature of such an act? Consideration of that question has occasioned considerable discussion about the relation of faith to reason. Some people see an opposition between the two; others, by far the majority of Christians, and the overwhelming majority of Anglicans, see not only compatibility but mutual aid between them.

If we consider faith and revelation from the point of view of the definition of religion we have used, we may say that revelation, stressing the initiative of God, is the ultimate reality Christians recognize, and that faith is the life-response made to that recognition. Faith and revelation require and influence each other. Understanding faith as a life-response means that a whole person, not just an isolated faculty, or part of a person, is involved. Faith, in other words, is not just an act of will, nor an act of reason, nor a feeling; it is not mere intellectual assent to formal doctrine. If what we have said about revelation is true— that it is God personally revealing himself to us—faith is the means of recognizing and accepting a Person rather than the means of accepting a proposition. Thus, faith involves our whole life as persons rather than only one of our abstract faculties within that life.

The Danish philosopher Sören Kierkegaard described faith as a "leap"; it is a way to get outside ourselves. If an Anglican had invented the metaphor, he would have called faith a "running broad jump." We have to leave our feet, as it were, in faith; that is to say, the object of faith is not something we can reach walking on the feet of our natural reason alone. Jumping is a new mode of transportation, and it depends upon an act of our will; in both of these respects "jumping" is useful in helping us understand faith, but the leap which is faith must not be made arbitrarily. It must be made in the direction our reasonable lives are running.

As we have indicated, Christians believe God always acts first in his relations with us. Everything in the Christian life is a response to God's call; we initiate nothing. We may be mistaken about a call, and, in the echo chamber we know as the world, we may not be sure from which direction a call is coming, but the only reason any sane person would leave his feet and commit himself to a jump is because he feels he will have a firm place to land. Faith must be reasonable!

Faith is the way we open ourselves to God; it is the way we respond to God, and God is different from the world. It was because of God's difference, the way his mystery escapes all representation and limitation, that idolatry was so consistently condemned in Judaism.

God cannot be seen, and when faith is described in Scripture, it is especially related to something unseen. The Hebrews, unlike the Greeks, did not think that seeing was the highest faculty of human beings; hearing was the most important ability for the Hebrews, for by hearing they could receive God's commandment.

That is a valid insight for, although we say "I see" when we understand something, the world of human culture is more a world of language and words than it is of sight. The subtle distinctions we are capable of making by means of words are what make our dictionaries so thick and our world so rich. We can make many more distinctions through combinations of words than we are capable of discerning with our naked eyes. A blind person enters human society much more easily than a deaf and mute person, a truth which is only too easily illustrated in some base humor. It is much easier to ridicule a deaf and mute person, than it is a blind person, for deaf and mute people do not seem quite as human as we are; the blind are more spontaneously accepted as unfortunate human beings. They are more immediately in the human world of words.

Because of God's difference from us, he cannot be seen by us, but the spiritual forefathers of Christianity believed he could be heard. He spoke to his people, Israel, in the Old Testament through "men of God," prophets, teachers, psalmists, and others with special *callings*. "Hear O Israel," is the way God addresses his people through Moses at the giving of the Law in the book of Deuteronomy (5,6). While recounting a moment of God's most intimate presence with his people, Moses recalls that "the Lord spoke to you out of the midst of fire: you heard the sound of words, but saw no form; there was only a voice" (Dt 4:12). Christians accept Jesus as the Word of God.

When it is said that human beings are created in the image of God, the image referred to is not the shape of the human body; it is the ability of a person to respond reasonably and freely to God's Word. That response is also called faith, and we can easily see that reason is not something external to it, approaching it from the outside. In a cacophony of worldly voices, reason works intrinsically in our listening as we try to discern which voice is God's and try to discern the message of the voice we finally concentrate upon.

An image makes no command. It issues no imperative. God does both. An image, in the sense in which it is prohibited in Judaism and in the sense in which we are considering it now, can be viewed with detachment; one is able to step back from it, and the viewer always has it in his or her perspective. A command, on the other hand, puts us under judgment, and that is the way the God of Abraham, Isaac, and Jacob made himself known to his people. A god who does not command our attention and our life is not God. That is why people prefer idols to God; they are easier to live with, for we have to pay attention to them only when we want to and only in the way we want to.

Faith is a life to be lived rather than a judgment made in a library. Only the understanding of faith as such a life-response enables us to understand what Paul meant' when he said that "whatever does not proceed from faith is sin" (Rom 14:23). Faith is a life open to God, a life involving reason and will; sin results when a life is closed to God, but a closing which also involves reason and will.

In a masterful bit of analysis, Austin Farrer has convincingly shown that no one ever first locates a neutral God and then puts his faith in him. A "God of the hypothesis" is no God at all. Because faith is a free and reasonable response to what a person perceives as a call, faith is commitment. It would be wrong to think that such commitment as we are identifying with faith is restricted to what would normally be recognized as religious faith. Farrer, as many others, points out that life itself is faith, that is, commitment to something. Everyone makes commitments, and the life of everyone of us is a jumble of commitments to one thing and another. We may relocate faith—direct it to new objects—but we never get faith in a vacuum. When such a relocation occurs, from the new point of view, a person is said to "get faith" for the first time.

An understanding of the situation such as Farrer suggests enables us, once again, to see that reason always plays its role from within faith. The abstract, critical work of reason always occurs within commitments that precede it. Everything we do is a response to some aspect of reality we hear calling to us. When that reality is ultimate enough to be called "God," we say that we are exercising religious faith. The real problem of faith is not that it is so rare but that so many people are religiously exercising faith in something less than God. Marxist atheism is as much a matter of faith as Christianity; it is just that the gods—the understanding of ultimate reality—are different. Reason is the means we use to choose between deities, and that decision is always made within some kind of faith commitment.[2]

William James, in his 1901 Gifford Lectures, said that one of the primary marks of religion is that it must be taken seriously. The point is not different from the one we have just been considering, for everyone is serious about something. We are serious about money, diets, politics, golf, and ourselves. Our problem is to be serious about, and have commitment to, the right thing. How can such a determination be made? By asking questions. By probing to see whether or not it is reasonable to take something as seriously as we do.

We have seen that there is no question as to whether or not there is religion in the world; the question is about the adequacy of the gods that compete for our attention. But once we begin asking questions about the adequacy of the gods other people— and we—are committed to, we must ask every question we can in order to be as reasonable as possible. We must not end our inquiry with one question left. We can—and must— question the reasonableness of the existence of God himself.

"Is there a God?" is a question religious people should ask

themselves. To be sure, the question will be asked from within their practice of religion, but that means only that they will ask the question best, for every question is asked in a context, and the context of religion is seriousness. We must have concern for a problem before we can fully hear and understand an answer to it. The same words mean more to us at one time than at another time because of the different backgrounds we have at the different times we hear the words. From a teacher's point of view, it is aggravating to have students ask what appears to be the same question over and over again in a course, but if a question was not *mine* when it was asked earlier, the answer was not mine when it was given.

No one begins asking questions from scratch or confronts bare reality with a bare mind, not even a skeptic, although skeptics may try to make us think so. But a skeptic lives in every believer, for both skeptics and believers live in a common world, and that world offers evidence that can make it difficult either to believe or not to believe. Wars, sickness, natural disasters, and the whole catalog of human hostility Christians call "sin" make it more than reasonable to ask whether or not anything like a personal and caring God could exist. The one thing Christianity has never asked its followers to do is to believe something even though it was not true—even the existence of God.

Christians believe in God because they are convinced that God has revealed himself to them in his Son. But the God who is believed to have spoken in the Son is also accepted as the God who created the physical universe. The one God may have expressed himself differently in what has been called the general revelation of his creation and in the special revelation of his Son, but the one truth of the one God cannot contradict itself in anything God does. From time to time in the history of Christianity, small groups have tried to maintain that the material world came from a source less than God, but such views have always been condemned by the Church as heretical.

Granting that difficulties to belief exist in the world, when asked whether or not it is reasonable to accept the existence of a God in the face of our knowledge of the world, Christians have always answered, "Yes." Christians say that God exists because of what they know about the world, not to compensate for what they do not know. God's existence is not a summation of human ignorance; his existence is the ground and consequence of the knowledge we have. Still, the knowledge of his existence is knowledge of a special kind.

One way to approach this kind of knowledge is through the remark of a well-known professor in Cambridge, England, whose special interest was logic and the critique of language. In his *Tractatus Logico-Philosophicus*, Ludwig Wittgenstein says that, "It is not the *how* of the existence of the world that is mystic, but the *fact* that it exists" (Proposition 6:44). That remark, made by a twentieth-century, non-Christian philosopher, can lead us to central currents in the thought of Western Christendom that provide the context of Hooker's reasonable approach to, and defense of, the faith that so characterized Anglican theological reaction to Puritan attacks.

The contention of the remark we have quoted is that the principal mystery confronting human beings does not concern the scientific description of how the changes which go on in the world occur. To be sure, there appear to be an unlimited number of questions about how the universe works, but our scientific observations and theories have gone a long way in helping us describe how nature operates. The bigger mystery Wittgenstein refers to requires a higher vantage point than that of physical science to see, for, instead of asking detailed questions about how this or that works, the larger mystery concerns the question *why* there is anything at all.

Our natural sciences begin with the fact that the universe exists; scientific activity then tries to describe how change occurs within the universe as it is given. But it is possible to ask the more basic question "why" about the fact that the universe exists at all. Is there any reason for its existence? Why does the universe exist with its present laws instead of some other mutually consistent set of principles? Traditional Western thought, going back to the time of Aristotle, distinguishes two types of questions. There are questions about *fact*, which ask *whether* something exists or not, and there are questions about the *reasoned fact*, which ask *why* something exists. If we push reason to its limits, we always want answers to questions about the reasoned fact, rather than merely the fact, for after we know that something is we want to know why it is. Science can answer questions about how things occur within the universe, but its descriptive method will not allow it to answer the question of why there is a universe.

The reasonableness of religion can be shown only if we persist in asking every legitimate question we can about the universe. It is religion, not science, which must push reason to the limit and ask the final question: why is there anything at all? "Why" is the basic question of the intellect. Children drive their parents mad by their persistence in asking the question, but the parents will be led to God if they try to answer the question wherever it can legitimately be asked. The one legitimate requirement for the question "why" is that there be some complexity in the subject about which the question is asked. We can ask why the ball is blue or why the footstool is here, or why there is any footstool at all; in every case we are asking why two aspects of reality that need not be together are found together. Nothing in the nature of being either a ball or being blue requires that they be found together, and there is nothing in the nature of a footstool that requires it to exist, so when "blue" and "ball" and "footstool" and "existence" are found together we can ask why that is the case.

Wherever we look in the being of the universe—including its being as a whole—we discover complexity. Atomic complexity permeates the universe; we discover an intelligible order in natural things unable to account for the order they have; the being of the universe does not satisfy the needs we ourselves have within it. We can ask the question "why" about all of these complexities, but the only final answer to that question can be found in the existence of some kind of reality about which such questions cannot be asked, yet which is itself the Source of everything else.

The way the conclusion we have just reached has been traditionally put is to say that the being of the universe is contingent—that is, we can always ask the question "why" about it—while the being of God is necessary. Because the being of the universe is contingent (composite), the ultimate reason why it is as it is must always be sought beyond it. The ultimate Source of the universe, which answers the final question about why the universe is as it is, cannot be contingent being. It must be necessary Being; which is to say, the question "why" cannot be asked about it because it does not have the type of composition about which questions can be asked.

Human beings do not know what necessary Being is like in itself. The only thing we can say about it is that it must exist if the existence of the universe is to be reasonable rather than arbitrary. We can have, at best, only a negative knowledge about such a different kind of Reality; we know better what it is not than what it is. St. Thomas Aquinas himself made that very point when he said that "because we cannot know what God is, but rather what he is not, we have no means for considering how God is, but rather how he is not."[3]

Put in perhaps more familiar terminology, it is usually said that God is the cause of the universe, but that nothing causes God. In traditional terms, it is said that the universe is being *ab alio*, from another, while God is being *a se*, being by itself. The latter phrase is sometimes mistakenly translated to say that God is "from himself," that God is "self-caused," but that would make God self-contradictory and irrational. As cause, God would have to be active, and, as effect, God would have to be passive; if he were self-caused, he would have to be active and passive at the same time in the same respect. A contradiction! God is not self-caused; he is the kind of reality that needs no cause, for, as we have seen, there is not the kind of composition in him (as there is in the universe) which needs an explanation. God is Reality which must be. There is no alternative to him.

We have just given in a summary fashion what is classically known as a "proof for the existence of God." Many people believe that the existence of God cannot be proved, and great portions of the history of Western philosophy and theology have been occupied with arguments about whether God's existence can be proved or not, and, if it can, how it can best be done. Some of those who believe that God's existence cannot be proved are correct, if their understanding of "proof" is accepted. They believe such an attempted proof is a "logical proof," and it is true that the existence of God cannot be proved by logic alone. That is not to say, however, that the existence of God is illogical. Quite the contrary. It is to say that logic is no more than a system of ideas and that God is much more than just an idea in the mind!

Another mistake often made in discussing the possibility of proving God's existence is to think that a proof for the existence of God begins in this world and ends outside this world. Actually, a proof for the existence of God begins in this world and ends in this world. We end where we begin, but with a different understanding of where we began. A proof of God's existence is more in the nature of a fundamental apprehension of reality in its basic existence than it is a logical process. Such a "proof" requires that we pay attention to the most immediate and fundamental experience of reality we can have; within the immediate, personal apprehension of that reality the "proof" tries to show that what is most real for us, the existence everything in the universe must have to make it real, refers beyond itself to some being-which-must-be, if reality is not basically absurd. The sequence of thought we have described does not consciously occur within the *immediate* apprehension of which we are speaking, but the structure can be drawn from the apprehension by later reflection upon it.

At this moment we should probably recall again that no one sits down with a blank mind and a blank piece of paper to decide in a vacuum whether or not there is a God in which to believe. Religion existed and a claimed knowledge of the living God existed long before anything like "proofs" for the existence of God were thought of. The need for "proofs" came up within religious lives that were being lived rather than first appearing in a world which had no religion and thought it would like one—if God existed.

In the portion of the *Summa Theologica* in which Aquinas gives his statements of the proof of the existence of God, he ends every statement with a variation of "and this everyone understands to be God...This all men speak of as God."[4] Critics of St. Thomas have said that in concluding his proofs by such statements, the great theologian acknowledged that the proofs were inconclusive; rather, what the statements show is that Aquinas was better aware of the total human situation than his critics understood. He knew that with the proofs he was providing a service for those who already believed—making it possible for them to continue to believe—rather than persuading people who had never heard of God to believe in God.

Rational analysis shows that the basic fabric of the universe has a complexity for which the universe itself cannot account; only a different kind of being from the universe can supply the reason for such being. The way religious language normally puts the matter is to say that the universe is created.

The doctrine of creation is another Christian belief about which a good deal of misunderstanding has arisen. As Fundamentalists and scientists are this day fighting about "creation science" and whether or not religion and science must contradict each other, we may go on briefly to consider what the doctrine of creation actually maintains. Part of the difficulty, once again, comes from the understanding of a Latin phrase, this time, *ex nihilo*.

Traditional Western thought states that God creates the universe *ex nihilo*, that is, "out of nothing." The literal translation of the Latin phrase makes it sound as if "nothing" were "something" out of which God made things. But "nothing" is not some kind of stuff the way wood is; thus, God did not make the universe "out of nothing" in a manner similar to the way a desk is "made out of wood."

To say that God created the universe *ex nihilo* is only a way of saying that the universe is *totally* or *completely* dependent in its reality on a kind of being different from it. Above all, we must understand that the religious doctrine of creation does not pretend to be a description of how God made the universe; it is simply the statement of the fact that the universe depends on God. The supposed battle between science and religion on the theory of evolution is a mistaken battle. Evolution does not explain God's act of creation. Evolution is only a description of how certain change occurs within the universe. In fact, evolution, the theory that radically new species of being arise from older, simpler kinds of being, itself requires an explanation if it is to be completely rational. Qualitatively new species may follow simpler species in time, but the new cannot come *from* the old in the sense of receiving newness from the very being that lacked newness in the past. As a temporal *description* of a certain kind of change, the theory of evolution has more to commend it than any other theory available to us, but it is a description rather than an explanation. Evolution requires something beyond it to account for the newness which arises within it.

The Christian doctrine of creation states that God is intimately present in his creation, enabling it to exist, but the doctrine does not try to describe how the act of creation occurs. The important thing is that if the world totally depends upon God at any one moment for its existence, it totally depends upon God for that existence every subsequent moment of its life. If my knife totally depends upon my hand to hold it in a given place in space for an instant, it totally depends upon my hand to keep it there as long as it remains in that place. If I withdraw my hand, the knife falls. In an analogous way, the universe depends for its existence upon God; thus God, although a different type of reality from the universe, is intimately present throughout the universe sustaining it in being—if the existence of the universe is rational.

The possibility of miracles arises precisely because of God's causal presence in his creation. There may have been a time when the existence of God was thought to be demonstrated by the existence of miracles, but, if so, that time is past; now the acceptance of miracles depends upon the prior acceptance of the existence of God. We are prohibited from going into the "problem of miracles" in any detail in the theological summary contained in this chapter, but we can ask, if there is a God who sustains creation at each moment of its existence, whether or not he could achieve his special purposes in a special way within creation. God works through nature, but he can also add his special purposes to nature. So viewed, miracles are not a contradiction of the laws of nature, for adding God's special purpose to nature is a way of constituting a new cause which can produce a new effect without contradiction.

An acknowledgment of the primacy of history in relation to abstract thought is crucial to the possibility of miracles, as that same acknowledgment is crucial in understanding the life of a human person. Our personal lives are constituted by singular, historical events which are incapable of being repeated for laboratory experimentation. There is something unique about human expression each time it occurs; the same must be said about miracles and God's revelatory expression through them.

Christianity depends on only one miracle, the resurrection

of Jesus from the dead. If the truth of Jesus' resurrection falls, all falls; if it stands, nothing more is necessary. If God exists, he exists before we know him, and he can accomplish his will without our understanding how he does it. Still, his truth is consistent wherever it is revealed, so nature and miracle cannot contradict each other.

Scientific insights, especially in quantum mechanics, have provided an understanding of nature in which the occurrence of such singular events as may be called miracles is much more reasonable than it was on older scientific views. In subatomic physics, the uniformity of nature is no longer thought of as a totally determinate mechanical system. At the heart of physical matter the same type of historical time which is the means by which persons express themselves—time in which singular events occur that cannot be reversed and experimented with—has been discovered. Religious conclusions cannot immediately be deduced from that discovery, but the openness of the physical world to God's presence in an historically significant manner can no longer be said to contradict science. Science, by its own methodology, has rediscovered the primacy of history.[5]

Ever since our initial remarks about the general nature of religion and our discussion of revelation, we have been discussing the nature of a reality that is independent of us and considering how we are able to talk about that reality. Looking at our life in the world and the long evolution of the universe that occurred before we appeared within it, a primacy must be admitted for the reality into which we are born, one that does not depend upon us in order to exist. Besides the existence of the world and the evolving universe, the existence of God is another reality that does not depend upon us.

But once we do exist, a correlation develops between us and the reality that exists independently of us. It is we who know reality, and that reality exists consciously for us only to the extent that we know it. Although external reality is different from us, it is *we* who must recognize that difference. The personal, embodied existence we have in a given time and place, therefore, is the key to the existence of everything else we know—even the existence of the farthest galaxies and the most rarified distinctions we can make in scientific abstractions.

Because of the situation we are describing, our thought processes—and the language in which our thoughts are expressed—are called upon to do some very difficult things: they must be able to describe reality insofar as it is different from us, as well as be able to describe it in its likeness to us. Language is at its clearest when it describes the kind of reality we are. In a profound sense, language is an extension of our bodies, for it is a way we "handle things." The most precise languages we know are abstract ones we invent, as in mathematics. In these languages, the terms are defined completely for our purposes, and the terms are used only as we have defined them. Such languages are totally without equivocation; they are univocal in meaning and illustrate the most precise human speech possible. The basic tables of multiplication and division are examples.

Even in the everyday world out of which our language grows, however, the reality of the world is too rich for language alone to capture. Every statement we make excludes something from our attention. If I describe something green, I abstract from all other colors; and if I describe something which is here, I leave out of consideration things that are everywhere else. It is the richness of reality, the richness left out of our precise but abstract scientific languages, that is responsible for the special use of language we know as poetry. Poetic expression lacks the clarity and precision of science, but it communicates dimensions of reality that truly exist, even though their existence escapes scientific description. The bloom of a rose and the bloom of a lover's cheek are totally lost to geometry.

The closer we get to the actual differences found in concrete reality, the more difficult it gets for language clearly to describe that reality. The total abstraction from all considerations except quantity allows us to understand that one arithmetic unit plus another arithmetic unity equals precisely two such units. When we use $1 + 1 = 2$ as part of the process of counting a dozen eggs in a box, no imprecision is added, although we are now talking about eggs instead of just numbers. But when we say $1 + 1 = 2$ and we are referring to two people in love, poetry rather than arithmetic will furnish the more satisfactory language. In the case of persons in love, we cannot abstract a single feature from the two people and think that that enables us to examine their love more clearly. William loves Meryl in her totality. When two people are in love, each person is so special to the other that nothing less that the physical presence of the other person will do. The poetic language of love is not as precise as arithmetic, but it is more human—and more moving for that very reason. It indicates more of the kind of being we are. We are better at feeling what it is to be in love than we are at feeling what it is to be a number; in fact, we are rightly insulted if someone thinks of us as no more than a number.

When human language tries to describe a reality as different from us as God must be if he is to be God, human language meets its supreme challenge. Such language must be used in a special way, but, as we have tried to indicate, such uses of language are necessary even in nature when persons are most fully human in their communication with each other. So it is that people in love write poetry. God's difference from us must never be compromised by the way we speak about him, and that means that the language we use to refer to him will always be imprecise and unclear. Still, since God has created us, we should be able to say something about him.

We know that we cannot have the type of clear and univocal knowledge about God that we have about mathematical units in arithmetic; we cannot use words to refer to God and to the natural world of which we are a part with equal precision. On the other hand, we should not be reduced to mere metaphor when we talk about God either. Metaphors make only accidental comparisons between things; they give no literal information. We learn for example, nothing literal about what it is to be a human child when a mother calls her crying baby "my poor lamb." But there is a third type of predication, which is neither as clear as univocal meaning nor as misleading as metaphorical meaning; it is analogical meaning. In it, one cannot make the total abstraction which allows for univocal meaning, but we can do better than the equivocal meaning we get from metaphors. Analogy is based upon what has been called "imperfect abstraction": it describes similarity in the midst of difference. Analogy can convey knowledge, for it can say something essential about what is being discussed, but it cannot convey the clearest knowledge possible, for it cannot completely abstract from the differences of the things being discussed. Everything it says is qualified by difference. Mary in her existence is not precisely the same as Betty in her existence, but Mary's existence is to her life analogically similar to Betty's existence to her life; there is similarity in the midst of difference.

Analogical knowledge is the only kind of knowledge we can have of God. When we speak of God's knowledge, we do not know what that knowledge is like in itself, but, by analogy we can say that God's knowledge is to his Being as our knowledge is to our being. The ability to use such statements about God is ultimately grounded on the fact that God is creator of the world. Since God created persons who have knowledge, God must somehow have in himself the perfections we see in his creation. We do not know what those perfections are like in him because we cannot completely abstract those perfections from the difference in his Being which makes him God, but we can see—dimly—that the role knowledge plays in our lives is somehow similar to the role his knowledge plays in his life. The knowledge we are able to have of God in this way enriches our appreciation of his mystery; it does not explain his mystery away.

Speaking of mystery, we must conclude this chapter with a reference to what, in a most profound sense, is the summation of the Christian mystery—the triune nature of God, for Christians believe that the one God is a Trinity of Persons.

Of all the doctrines of Christianity, the doctrine of the Trinity is the one we are least tempted to believe was concocted by human reason alone. There is no philosophical path to it. Christians believe that God is triune for one reason only: they believe it because of the primacy of history; they believe the truth to be historically revealed in the sending of Jesus Christ. Christians accept Jesus as the human expression of the deepest mystery of God; they accept Jesus as the way God expresses himself in human nature. Jesus is God's Word, and that Word is nothing less than God himself existing with God as God before anything else came into being. "In the beginning was the Word, and the Word was with God, and the Word was God" (Jn 1:1). When that Word is spoken as Jesus, God uses humankind for his, God's, purposes, rather than human beings seeking God for their purposes.

In their historical experience of God in Jesus, believers also learn that God is love, and they experience the gift of that love in the gift of the Spirit.

The historical experience of the first Christians is the only foundation for Christians' lives with the God they worship. Austin Farrer, former Warden of Kebel College at Oxford, stresses the unique nature of the revelation of the Trinity in a different manner, but in a manner eminently historical and biblical. He argues against trying to theorize and conceptualize the trinitarian life of God as that life has been revealed to us. He suggests that the revelation of God in Christ proceeds through "images" rather than through "concepts." The "kingdom of God" and the "Son of Man" are two images which interpret events; the doctrine of the Trinity is another such image, according to Farrer, and we "fall into absurdity," he maintains, when we try to make conceptual inferences from the images.

Images, rather than concepts, are helpful to us in our relations with God, because the concreteness of images requires that they be lived rather than just thought; they make an appeal to the whole person, in other words, stimulating both our reason and our will. Images of the Trinity are found in the Gospel accounts of the baptism of Jesus, where the voice of the Father calls Jesus, "Son," and the Spirit descends upon Jesus as a dove. In the book of Revelation (with an imagery first found in Isaiah 11), the Trinity is seen in "the Father, the sevenfold Spirit before his throne, [and in] the Son on whom the whole Spirit is bestowed."[6] The Christian doctrine of God is neatly and incisively summarized, again according to Farrer, in one simple sentence: "The act of paternal love is twofold—to beget and to bestow."[7]

In the revelation of God given through Jesus Christ, philosophical deductions are out of place. Conceptual deductions about how the Persons of the Trinity are related to each other and how they proceed from each other have been offered from time to time in both Eastern and Western Christendom. In the West the nature of deity, a nature common to all three Persons, is the point of origin; in the East, the primacy of the Father is the source of such deductions. All such deductions are presumptuous! The basic doctrine of the Trinity begins with the threefold communion of Persons already existing as the one God; the first step in trying to describe how that is able to be the case is already a step too far.

"God is love," the First Letter of John tells us (4:8). That revelation in Jesus is where the Christian knowledge of God begins, not where it ends. Taking that revelation seriously, as, according to William James, one should take every religious statement, the doctrine of the Trinity, although not understood, may nevertheless be seen not to be absurd. Love, even as we know it in this world, is a union of persons. Love requires at least two persons to be itself, but, being a unity of persons, it overcomes their separation at the very moment it intensifies their distinction. A person never feels more himself than when he is in love, yet love is a union with someone else!

If God only *has* love, then there must be composition between him and the object of his love—for then God needs something outside of himself to love and he is dependent upon something beyond himself to be himself. That is precisely the way "process theology" argues in our day. If God *is* love, however, as the Christian revelation maintains, no object less than God would be an adequate object for his love. If God *is* love, the structure which allows love to be itself must somehow be found within God. Christians believe God has revealed himself to be such a community, a community of self-expression and love, of begetting and bestowing. In that view, creation is truly an act of love; it is a free act, something God did not have to do. Human re-creation—redemption—in Christ is a free act of love also. That is why a freely given return of love to God by us is the only adequate response to the God in whom Christians believe.

3

Jesus Christ:
God With Us

James E. Griffiss

In corporate worship Anglicans regularly say the Apostles'
Creed or the Nicene Creed as part of their offering of praise and
thanksgiving. In doing so they confess their belief in Jesus
Christ, the only Son of God, who became a human being, a man,
for our salvation, who died upon the Cross, and who was raised
to the glory of the Father. Confession of faith in Jesus Christ as
Savior and Lord is central to the creeds of the Church, and it is a
belief which has formed the tradition of Anglican doctrine and
practice, worship and prayer. It is also at the center of the
everyday lives of those who seek to be followers in the way of
Jesus. The confession of faith has taken many forms, and all of
them have involved a long history of theological reflection,
explanation, and justification, not only by Anglicans but by
countless other believers in the Christian Church. The question,
Who is Jesus and how is he our Savior and Lord? has been
answered in the technical language of theology and philosophy
as well as in simple words of prayer to him and worship in his
name, through acts of justice and mercy, and in a sacrificial life
of service to others. The answers have varied considerably in
Christian history, reflecting the times and circumstances of

believers, the degree of their commitment to Jesus Christ, and their understanding of what they believe he calls them to be and to do. Beneath all of the answers, however, is the experience of him as one who saves, who makes people whole, and who calls and directs us to the God he called Father. That experience of salvation is at the heart of belief in Jesus Christ, however it may be expressed.

While there is no one doctrine of Christ that can be called typically or uniquely Anglican, there have been, I believe, certain factors in our history which have formed and structured our life in Christ, and so our way of talking about him. Those factors have derived from the pattern of worship we have known in the *Book of Common Prayer*: the ordered reading of Holy Scripture, the regular recitation of the ancient creeds, and the centrality of Baptism and the Eucharist. How Christians worship reflects what they believe, and it affects the way they formulate their beliefs. In this essay on Christology, I shall explore one way in which an Anglican can talk about belief in Jesus Christ out of our pattern of worship: Scripture, Creeds, and Sacraments, as they have enabled me and, I trust, many others to come to know the saving work of God in Christ.

The Question of Jesus Christ

That people have responded in faith to Jesus Christ is the presupposition of Christology. If he were not a person in whom people have believed, he would be only another figure in the past about whom it might be interesting and even important to know something, such as how he lived, what he said, and what people thought of him. There are many such figures. Socrates, for example, can be for the student of philosophy a figure commanding great respect and admiration, a person about whom it is important to know as much as possible, one in whose teachings we may believe, holding them to be true; but we do not ordinarily say that we believe in Socrates or have faith in him as Christian people have said about Jesus of Nazareth. There is something about Jesus, as he was remembered and proclaimed in the New Testament and as he is still proclaimed today, that has led those who believe in him to call him Savior and Lord, to pray to him, and to believe him to be a continuing presence in their lives.

Christology, or theological reflection upon the life and significance of Jesus, is the attempt to say why it is that people can use such language about him and what that language means. In other words, it is concerned with the question, Who is Jesus?, but it is driven to ask the question not simply out of curiosity about a figure in the past, but because people have believed in him and have described their belief in him in certain ways. Those who believe in Jesus and who are thus driven to ask questions about him, do so because he puts a question to them and to all human beings. Those who heard and followed Jesus frequently put questions to him; they asked him to explain himself and they wanted to know the source of his authority. But Jesus, as he is remembered and witnessed to in the New Testament, turned the questions back. He asked his disciples, "Who do you say that I am ?" In asking such a question he was asking them—as he is us—who are we who ask him questions about himself. The "question of Jesus," then, has several dimensions: Who is he, who do we say he is, and who are we who can—and do—ask such questions? Christology is concerned with all these matters.

The story in which Jesus puts to his disciples the question, "Who do you say that I am?" appears in all of the Gospels (Mk 8:27-33 and parallels; cf. Jn 6:66), and it calls forth the response from Peter, which has been termed the first christological confession: "You are the Christ, the Anointed One of God." But that story, as important as it is, needs to be seen in a larger context; it is not a story to be told in isolation from the total ministry of Jesus. Jesus' question is implicit in everything said about Jesus in the gospel traditions and in the other writings of the New Testament. Indeed, the whole of the New Testament can be thought of as the attempt to answer the question that Jesus puts to men and women by his actions and his teaching. Jesus spoke and acted with an authority that could not be accounted for by calling him a prophet or by comparing him to other persons who had spoken or acted for God in the history of the Jewish people.

But even more important than the teaching and actions of Jesus was a quality in him pointed to over and over again in the gospel traditions. Those who came into contact with him were called to change their lives, to repent and believe, and to prepare for the Kingdom God had promised to his people. In some traditions Jesus was remembered as the one who proclaimed the Kingdom, in others as the one in whom the Kingdom has drawn near. It is not just what he says and does that is important. That he was believed by those who knew him to have a special, even unique relationship to the Promise of God's Kingdom gives to the gospel accounts of his ministry a particular urgency: Who is this Jesus who tells stories about God's way of dealing with people and who acts in such a way that people must respond to him not just as another teacher but as one in whom God's Promise has drawn near? And as we know from the Gospels the question he put to those who came into his presence called forth different reactions. Some believed in him and continued to follow him; others turned away.

It was his death and resurrection that gave focus to all of the memories of the words and actions of Jesus and that raised to a new level the question he had put to those who had known him. His death and resurrection called for answers that went far beyond those that could have been given during the time of his ministry. Early Christian preaching in the Gospels and in the letters of Paul and the book of Acts and the later theological reflection of the Gospel of John make it clear that the death and resurrection of Jesus was seen as proof that his relationship with God went far beyond the Old Testament categories and images through which Judaism could understand him, and far beyond the categories and images common to the gentile world to which he was preached: Jesus as the risen Christ spoke for God, revealed him in a way that was previously unknown, and represented him in a new and radical way. In the risen Christ, the early Christians claimed, God's nature was revealed as grace and truth (John), as love (the epistles of John), as the one who freely justifies sinners (Paul), as the one who is Lord and Savior of the Gentiles as well as the Jews (Luke/Acts). The preaching of the Cross and Resurrection put the question posed by Jesus himself in a new perspective and radically challenged the assumptions of Jews and Greeks about God and man.

For the Jews, who had a long history of involvement through the Covenant with the God whom they called Lord, to claim that the God of Abraham, Isaac, and Jacob had come to his people in the life of a particular human being, one who could speak with an authority greater than that of Moses and the prophets, who could be crucified by Roman power and yet, in his resurrection be the Anointed One, the promised Messiah of God, and that in him the Kingdom had come was blasphemy. But early Christian preaching about the crucified and risen Christ spoke of the God the Jews knew through the Law and the Covenant and the prophets in a manner which opened up new possibilities of knowing him and living according to the Law. It spoke of a new Covenant, not replacing, but fulfilling and transforming, the Covenant in which Judaism had lived and had come to know God's holiness, transcendence, and righteousness. The Letter to the Hebrews, for example, provides one of the most sustained attempts in the New Testament to open up the Jewish idea of God to what was being shown of him in Jesus. There the God of Moses and the prophets is described as the God of peace "who brought again from the dead our Lord Jesus, the great shepherd of the sheep, by the blood of the eternal covenant" (Heb 13:20ff). The Letter draws together in Jesus the fundamental images of Israel's history as a covenant people.

For the Gentiles, to whom Jesus was also represented as the crucified and risen Lord, the claim that he was the presence of God in human history posed a question less startling in one sense and more so in another. The Greco-Roman world knew of theophanies—the temporary appearance of the gods in sacred places or in a human form. If the God of Judaism was awesome in his holiness, righteousness, and transcendence, the deities of many of the popular gentile religions were all too familiar. As we can see from the book of Acts, the Gentiles could accommodate to their own religions the healing and miracles done in the name of Jesus and they could call Barnabas and Paul by the names of their own gods (14:8ff). What was startling in the preaching about Jesus was the belief that the eternal and ruling principle of the cosmos should be present in the suffering and death of a man of flesh and blood—and that he should be raised from the dead. Paul, for example, insisted that God's free gift of salvation is made available to all men and women, Jews and Greeks, in the death of Jesus on the Cross, and he vigorously opposed the spiritualizing tendency of some early converts to seek wisdom and salvation elsewhere (cf. 1 Corinthians). Further, the Prologue to the Gospel of John, through its identification of Jesus with the Logos, radically transformed the philosophical understanding of God as a self-identical and self-contained first principle, one who could not be conceived of in terms of temporality and change.

The question Jesus put to those who knew him in his Palestinian ministry and to those to whom he was represented as the risen Christ was the question of God. As such it is a question with which those who believe in Jesus must always deal: What is the nature of the God whom he reveals? But he puts that question to those who believe in him (as well as to those who do not) in his existence as a man and a Jew, who lived a life in history with all the ambiguities and limitations of human existence. It is as a man and as a Jew that Jesus brings us into relationship with God, revealing the nature of God to us. For that reason the question Jesus puts to us about God is also a question about man—about all men and women who share in his humanity. In some ways, the question the humanity of Jesus poses for us is the most important of all, and I want to discuss one aspect of it as it appears in the New Testament. Jesus, as a man and a Jew and as the risen Christ, posed the question of salvation: What does it mean to be a human being for whom God cares?

For the earliest believers in Jesus, who were themselves Jews, the human existence of Jesus and his significance for others could be understood in terms traditional to Judaism, even though many of them had to be stretched in order to account for what he said and did. Jesus was called Son of Man, Messiah, Son of God, titles which could express how he brought God's salvation to the people of the Covenant. It is true that in some of the gospel traditions Jesus is shown as having concern for those outside the Covenant (e.g., the Samaritan woman [Jn 4]; the centurion's slave [Lk 7]; the association with Zacchaeus [Lk 19] and with the Syrophoenician woman [Mk 7]), and in some of the parables of the Kingdom he is shown as extending the call to God's Kingdom beyond the people of the Covenant (e.g., the Marriage [Mt 22 and LK 14]; the Pharisee and the tax collector [Lk 18]), and both of those aspects of Jesus ministry are important to our understanding of him.[1] But as we can see from the book of Acts many in the early Christian community continued to understand the significance of Jesus and the offer of salvation God extends through him only in terms of the Law and the Covenant. The earliest gentile converts were admitted into the Covenant people through circumcision and obedience to the Law (Acts 10, 11, 15). The Jew who believed in Jesus as the Promised One of God could understand him as the one in whom the Covenant had been fulfilled and made new, but not as a totally new offer of salvation. When, however, Paul, the Jew, turned to the Gentiles and revolutionized Jewish Christian belief in Jesus, he and others were required to deal with the fundamental question, How do those who are not Jews stand in regard to God and his Kingdom?

Paul's interpretation of the gospel of Jesus broke open the categories that governed the way both Jews and Gentiles understood themselves to be as human beings in relation to God. First, it required Jewish Christianity to recognize the universality of Christ's saving work, namely, that human beings are redeemed in Christ not by their becoming Jews through circumcision under the Law but by the free gift of God, which makes all people the children of God and heirs of his salvation. In the Letter to the Galatians Paul developed that theme with great power: "But when the time had fully come, God sent forth his Son, born of woman, born under the law, to redeem those who were under the law, so that we might receive adoption as sons. And because you are sons, God has sent the Spirit of his Son into our hearts, crying, 'Abba! Father!' So through God you are no longer a slave but a son, and if a son then an heir" (4:4-7).

For Paul, Jesus could be the savior of all, the one in whom God's free gift is offered, not because he and they were Jews but because all human beings fall under the condemnation of sin and stand in need of God's free gift of grace through faith: "Then what becomes of our boasting? It is excluded. On what principle? On the principle of works? No, but on the principle of faith. For we hold that a man is justified by faith apart from works of law. Or is God the God of Jews only? Is he not the God of Gentiles also? Yes, of Gentiles also, since God is one; and he will justify the circumcised on the ground of their faith and the uncircumcised through their faith" (Rom 3:27-30). In Jesus a new humanity has been created which transcends the old divisions and separations between Jews and Greeks, male and female, slave and free. As it developed in the early Christian community, Paul's theology of the saving work of Christ—that he is the eschatological Man, Second Adam, and the New Creation—opened the way for the Gentiles to be incorporated into Christ (cf. Ephesians 2:11-22). This way of thinking about Jesus and his saving works required the Christian community to deal more and more deeply with the question that the teaching and example, death and resurrection of Christ always pose: How do we call him Savior and Lord of all human beings?

There was another less direct but, in the end, perhaps, more important consequence of Paul's mission to the Gentiles and the Christology which developed out of that mission. Early Christian proclamation transformed the gods of the Gentiles by confronting them with the God who is made known in the Cross and Resurrection. In addition, it confronted the dominant religious assumptions and philosophical explanations about human nature in the Greco-Roman world in which Christ was preached, and in doing so it transformed the understanding of humanity that had developed out of the Greco-Roman religious and philosophical tradition. The tradition was a melange of philosophies and religions,[2] but there were certain common patterns in its understanding of human nature centered around a doctrine of the soul as an immaterial entity distinct from the body and from all material forms. For much of that religious and philosophical tradition (stemming largely from Platonism) the soul was conceived of as immortal and in and of itself capable of surviving the death of the body; it participated in a higher order of reality than that which characterized space and time. Salvation was thus thought of as a passage from the limitations of the flesh to union, in some form, with the higher principles of the cosmos, to be accomplished either through wisdom and the life of philosophical speculation or through initiation into the mystery religions which flourished in the first and second centuries. Paul's preaching of Christ to the Gentiles placed the Gospel in direct confrontation with such a world view. Paul confronted the gentile world with the radical nature of human sin for which the Cross is the only answer. His preaching of the Cross required that gentile Christians recognize they could rely only upon God's grace for their hope of salvation, and it ruled out the idolatry of human perfectibility and self-justification. Jews could not be justified by the law, nor could Gentiles find salvation through some strength or principle within themselves (cf. Romans 1, 2). Both Jews and Greeks could be saved only in the free gift of God offered to all in Jesus Christ.

The history of the Church shows clearly that Paul's way of interpreting human nature and the hope of salvation has not always been readily accepted. To some degree we have taken over the doctrine of the immortality of the soul, and there have been those who have understood the way to salvation as a growth in spiritual enlightenment which has little use for the materiality of the flesh. On the other hand, I believe the Pauline theology of sin and the Cross has been too dominant in some forms of western theology: other ways of understanding the saving work of Christ are also needed. But Paul did confront the gentile world at its center. By focusing upon sin and the Cross he put the question of Jesus in its sharpest form: What is it to be a human being who is saved by Jesus Christ?

That is still the question of Jesus, as we who believe ask it of him and, even more important, as he asks it of us: Who are you that in me you have known God's saving power? To put it another way, the question Who is Jesus? arises out of experience of salvation in him, and only as we explore that mystery can we approach (although never fully comprehend) the question which he put to Peter, Who do you say that I am?

Jesus Christ: God Incarnate

The New Testament is the first witness to Jesus Christ and the beginning of the christological tradition. In various ways it tells the story of what it is like to be met by Jesus and in him to experience salvation, healing, wholeness and freedom. It also offers various explanations about why one can—and should— experience such things in him. In other words, not only does it raise the question of Jesus, it also seeks to answer the question

Jesus puts to those who believe in him, and it proclaims him in order that others may also believe.

Today, it is almost a truism to say that the New Testament does not provide us with a biography of Jesus, nor does it give us an historical account of his life and teaching such as one might expect to find in a newspaper story about any prominent figure. But like all truisms, this one, too, needs repeating. The New Testament is a collection of writings by those who believed in Jesus; it draws together various remembered traditions about him, not in the tradition of "objective history" but in the inspiration of the one event that totally transformed how he was perceived, namely, his being raised from the dead and exalted to the Father, and his pouring out of his Spirit on those who believed. The New Testament is an interpretation of Jesus' resurrection and exaltation in the power of the Spirit. It is history remembered in terms of an event. That this is so has important consequences for the way in which the story of Jesus is told, how he is witnessed to, and how we who hear the words of Scripture understand what is being said to us.

The New Testament is faith speaking to faith: the witness of those who first believed in Jesus Christ and of the Church which came into existence in his resurrection and in the outpouring of the Spirit. Easter does not stand in isolation from Pentecost. In the Spirit the disciples could now *see* (that is, believe with understanding) him in a new way, namely in his relationship to the one he called Father. They were transformed into the community of faith and had a gospel to preach. Jesus, the historical figure they had known, the man and the Jew, was also the risen and exalted Christ. There is thus a tension in the New Testament itself between Jesus, the concrete, particular human being, one whose family was known, one who could be remembered, and the Jesus who transcends history in his resurrection, ascension, and exaltation. That is a tension with which Christians must always live, for it expresses the mystery of Christ. There have been occasions in the history of Christian spirituality and doctrine when the tension has been broken apart or dissolved. That happens when we forget the historical Jesus, the man and the Jew, and turn the story of his life into a gnostic redeemer myth. It also happens when we reduce him and his significance to only his historic life and say of him only what can be known about him in strictly historical terms. But the tension in the New Testament itself shows us that the Jesus who lived and died *is* the Christ, or, as E. Schillebeeckx has said, Christianity is not just the message or teaching of Jesus; it is the continuing proclamation of the "persisting eschatological relevance of his person itself."[3] To separate the Jesus of history from the Christ of faith is to lose the person to whom the New Testament bears witness and whose story it tells. The Jesus of history is the person who was remembered by those who, in him, experienced God's salvation, he whom they called the Christ.

For us today who hear and read the words of Scripture, that double dimension of the person of Jesus is of fundamental importance. The story of his life and death and his resurrection and exaltation are told to us in the New Testament; we can hear about those events as something which happened a long time ago. But for those who believe in Jesus as Savior and Lord, the events recounted in the New Testament are more than stories told about what happened many years ago. We who hear the stories now also stand in relationship to the Jesus about whom they are told. He is re-membered by us in the words of Scripture because we can recognize in the stories one who is active and present even now in the life of the community of faith. To believe in Jesus as the one who was raised from the dead and who has been exalted to the right hand of the Father, as we confess in the creeds, is not only to look back to a figure in the past, but also to know him in the present as Savior and Lord.[4]

Biblical witness to Jesus is important in the development of Christology. In the New Testament we are given several emerging Christologies, several ways of reflecting upon who Jesus is and what we must say about him because we experience salvation in him. New Testament scholars have pointed to at least two general patterns of development. The first, characteristic of the synoptic Gospels and the Pauline epistles, was fundamentally eschatological. Paul, for example, thinks of Jesus as the eschatological man, the one who is the prototype of all humanity, and he looks forward to the Christ who is to come again in order to fulfill and complete the work of redemption. Similar themes can be found in the synoptic Gospels: Jesus is interpreted as the

eschatological judge, the fulfillment of God's promised Kingdom, the one who brings in the Kingdom, and so forth. It would
seem that the earliest reflections about Jesus (which to a considerable degree may have reflected the actual message of Jesus
himself) centered on the important questions about what he
brings to pass and what the future holds because of him, not on
the question of his origin.

Such a way of understanding Jesus, however, involves a
further dimension, one which emerged most explicitly in the
later Pauline epistles (Ephesians and Colossians, especially, but
also Philippians in its use of Wisdom language) and in John's
Gospel, namely, the relationship of Jesus to the God he proclaimed in terms of his preexistence.[5] It can be argued, for
example, that for Paul the eschatological significance of the
resurrection led to a deeper understanding of Jesus as Cosmic
Lord. The Jewish titles used about him had to be broken open
and language about his relationship with God "in the beginning" began to emerge: Christ comes to be seen as "the
eschatological fulfillment of God's purpose from the beginning,
the revelation and resolution of God's ultimate mystery."[6] That
movement reached its culmination in the Gospel of John, where
the divine status and preexistence of Christ is explicitly
affirmed: "it is in the Logos poem of the Johannine prologue
that the Wisdom and Logos speculation of Alexandrian Judaism
reach their climax, with the explicit statement that the Logos,
God's creative and revelatory utterance from the beginning of
time, has become flesh, that Christ *is* and not merely speaks
God's word to man."[7]

More could be said about the pattern of christological
development in the New Testament—it is not an uncomplicated
subject about which all New Testament scholars are unanimous!
One thing of importance, however, does need to be said here.
The two patterns of development in the interpretation of Jesus
as a person and of his significance for those who believe in him
are not incompatible. They witness to him in ways that can be
distinguished from one another, but both reflect what Christians
have come to see as essential to their interpretation of him and
his significance. The encounter with Jesus and the experience of
salvation in him call for a language that can express the depth of

what we mean when we use the words God and man. His concreteness and historicity, his existence as a man and a Jew, required the new Testament community (as it requires us) to ask about his ultimate relationship with the God he called Father; but that relationship also required them (and us) to ask about his existence as man, as the one who is the full expression of what it is to be human. In Jesus, God's salvation is made present and freely available in a human life—that is the New Testament witness. To provide a language appropriate to that experience of salvation in Jesus is the task of christological reflection from the New Testament on.[8]

The struggle to find such a language is the history of the first five centuries of Christian theology. There were many lines of development; some proved to be inadequate and died out, while others did not catch the imagination of the early Church or were not able to deal with the cultural and philosophical milieu in which the Church existed. One pattern, however, did emerge as the clearly dominant way of talking about Jesus and his significance: Logos Christology. While it is perhaps unfortunate that some of the other patterns were not more fully developed in the early history of the Church (several of them are now receiving fuller development), Logos Christology did enable the Christian community to interpret Jesus in a manner that could challenge and expand the categories through which the Greco-Roman world thought of God and man, opening up many new possibilities for theological development in other areas of the *mysterium christi.*

The history of Logos Christology—from its beginning in John's Gospel, through the Apologists, culminating in the Chalcedonian definition—is complex. My concern here is not to recount that complex history,[9] but to point to several aspects of Logos Christology which are, I believe, important for what we call the doctrine of the Incarnation. In the Greek philosophical tradition Logos was the term used for the rational, ordered dimension of reality—both human and cosmic. Logos is word, concept, reason; it expresses the way we know things, but it also expresses the way things are. For the philosophical tradition out of which Logos theology developed, human beings can, in fact, know things because our act of mind (our logos) reflects or participates in the cosmic order itself. When the Prologue to the Gospel of John identified Jesus with the Logos it was identifying an itinerant Jewish preacher, crucified upon a cross, with the order and rationality of the cosmos. It was saying, in effect, that the intelligibility of all that is, the First Principle of Being, is now present in the man Jesus of Nazareth. There were two important and revolutionary dimensions to such an assertion: Jesus Christ who is the Logos, the eternal and creative Word of God incarnate in the flesh and blood of a human being, is both the mediator of salvation *and* the person who reveals to us the nature of God. God through the Logos redeems humanity in the man, Jesus; and Jesus the man in whom the Logos is incarnate is the one through whom we can come to a knowledge of the truth of all reality.

The identification of Jesus with the Logos of God, in the patristic period, led to two major controversies through which the language appropriate to talk about Jesus Christ as God incarnate was defined. The first, the Arian controversy, centered around that nature of the relationship between the Son or Logos and the Father. Essentially, the question the Arian controversy raised was, Is the Son and Logos, who is incarnate in Jesus, equal in every respect to the Father, sharing in the divine nature, or is the Son and Logos something less than the Father and so a being who cannot be called God? Arius, approaching the question from a philosophical tradition reluctant to involve the eternal and divine principle in the contingency of temporal existence (a point of view which manifested itself early in the history of Christianity), maintained that there must be a difference between the Father and the Son so as to preserve the absolute impassibility of God the Father. He and his followers argued that there was a time when the Son was not, and therefore that he could not share in the divinity of the Father; he was to be thought of as the firstborn of all creation but not as one who shares the divine nature from all eternity. Athanasius, the Bishop of Alexandria, who took up the battle for what eventually came to be the orthodox position, maintained against the Arians that the Son and Logos is of one being or substance with the Father—*homoousion*. There was much of a philosophical nature involved in the controversy, involving especially what was meant by the word *ousia*, that need not detain us here. Athanasius, however, did see clearly the nature of the problem in the Arian position, namely, if in Jesus we are not met by the true and eternal God, the Son and Logos, our salvation in Christ would not be real and effective.[10]

Although the controversy continued for many years—even for centuries (there were occasional outbreaks of Arianism in the West much later on), the Nicene Creed clarified and established one of the central affirmations of the New Testament witness to Jesus: that in him we have to do with the true presence of God. By doing so in terms of the consubstantiality of the Son and Logos with the Father it provided a terminology in which, eventually, Christian belief in God as Father, Son, and Holy Spirit could also be stated conceptually as the doctrine that God is one substance (*ousia*) in three persons (*hypostases*).

But the Nicean confession of the Son and Logos as "of one substance" with the Father brought into focus the problem and mystery of Jesus the man and his relationship to the eternal and divine Logos. That aspect of Logos Christology was important in the controversies that led to the Chalcedonian Definition, and it continues to be a vexed question even today in any christological discussion regarding the doctrine of the Incarnation as central to Christian belief. One form of Logos Christology in the patristic period (called "logos-sarx" Christology), in its reluctance to identify the divine principle with temporality, change, and death, essentially (although there were many subtleties of expression) meant by incarnation that the Logos took on flesh, that it, in effect, replaced the human soul of Jesus so that one could only speak of the personal identity of the man Jesus in terms of a unity of a body and the Logos itself. But as some of the Fathers saw, such an incarnation of the Logos could not be for our salvation; the salvation of human beings, they said, must involve not only the Logos and flesh but the wholeness or fullness of human nature, soul and body. "Logos-anthropos" Christology struggled to find a terminology that could express a real and significant relationship between the eternal Logos and a genuine human being. Through the many controversies in the period between Nicea and the Council of Chalcedon it came to be seen that the only way Jesus could be talked about as one who is Lord and Savior of all human beings is to say that his human nature is also consubstantial with ours.

The two schools of Antioch and Alexandria, with all of their differences, epitomize, in their period, the attempt to state clearly the belief that in Jesus we have to do with one who is both genuinely human and genuinely the presence of the eternal Son and Logos. The conflict that existed between the two schools is a conflict for which proponents of either side can still be found.[11] Even though we cannot resolve it here, the conflict itself may prove useful to us.

The Antiochenes were fundamentally concerned with preserving the integrity of the human existence of Jesus. Theodore of Mopsuestia, the Bishop of Antioch, for example, took with great seriousness the life of Jesus as it is shown to us in the Gospels, and he used images of the indwelling of the Logos in the man Jesus so that the Logos could be said to have assumed the life of a man: the man Jesus in his freedom as a human being is the *locus* of the Incarnation and the unity of the divine and human natures. Jesus, the man assumed, Theodore said, shares with the Logos "in all the dignity in which he who indwells, being Son by nature, participates."[12] We, now, through Baptism and Eucharist, share in his glory and dignity.

The concern to preserve the integrity of the human life of Jesus while at the same time recognizing the divine indwelling of the Logos was of great importance in the patristic period when Platonism, with its tendency to disparage or forget historical reality, was very much a dominant philosophical point of view. At the same time, however, the position of the Alexandrian school, especially Cyril of Alexandria in his polemic against Nestorius, was of equal importance for the development of the doctrine of the Incarnation. Through the maze of confused and conflicting terminology in the writings of the Fathers between Nicea and the Council of Chalcedon there can be discerned in the Alexandrian school a sense of the unity of God and man in Jesus Christ, which is also essential to the biblical witness. Cyril, the most forceful of the Alexandrians, in a theology that was far from static and that underwent many changes in terminology, attempted to say what Chalcedon would establish later in more precise terminology, namely, that Jesus as a person is the true presence of God in a human life, a presence of such a kind that the image of indwelling as used by the Antiochenes was inadequate to express the reality. For Cyril the human nature of Jesus, what he is as a man, finds its actual existence in the Logos; the humanity of Jesus through its union with the Logos does not cease to be human but becomes truly human through the personal unity of Logos and Man in the Incarnation: "God the Logos did not come into a man, but he 'truly' became man, while remaining God."[13]

The Chalcedonian Definition, in which the differing points of view of Antioch and Alexandria were brought into, at least, verbal agreement, both culminated and began a long development in the doctrine of the Incarnation. It culminated the patristic attempt to find a language adequate to answer the question put to us by the historical life of Jesus and his significance for those who believe in him as Savior and Lord, namely , that in him we are met by God the Logos in a genuinely human life. And it did so through a notion of personal or hypostatic unity. For Chalcedon the unity of God and Man in Jesus, his personal reality, is not to be found in the putting together of two disparate natures, as though we were mixing oil and water, but a unity *in* two natures. Jesus Christ, according to Chalcedon, is one person; in him we can discern the reality of God and the reality of man; he is the presence of divine transcendence in history, the God who is with us without ceasing to be God, who in Jesus commits himself to our humanity without restriction or reservation; he is God with us for our salvation. But he is present with us in such a way that Jesus shows us what it is to be truly human. The humanity of Jesus, that which we share with him, finds its center, its reality, in God; it expresses or reveals his unlimited unity with God, and thus shows us that our true existence as human beings is our unity with God. There were many subsequent interpretations of the Chalcedonian Definition, some of which, by defining the mystery of personal unity too precisely, obscured its essential witness. But the abiding contribution of Chalcedon to the doctrine of the Incarnation remains: in a truly human life God is with us for our salvation.[14]

Chalcedon, however, was also a beginning. Certainly it has remained as an authoritative teaching of the Church concerning the person and significance of Jesus, but it has had fruitful consequences in other areas as well. It enabled subsequent generations to develop a doctrine of the Church and of the sacramental life in which the real presence of God in human history could be expressed in terms of our calling into the divine life, our communion with God, and our divinization as sons and daughters of God. While that development is, perhaps, most prominent in the teaching of the Othodox Churches, it is also part of the western tradition, albeit, obscured from time to time. It has not been unimportant, for example, in Anglican thinking about the Church and the sacraments. Both Richard Hooker and Lancelot Andrewes in the sixteenth century took the doctrine of the Incarnation, as formulated by Chalcedon, to be the theological foundation for our sacramental participation in the humanity of Christ and the paradigm of our unity with God. In the nineteeth century, E. B. Pusey and others in the Oxford Movement, as well as B. F. Westcott and F. D. Maurice from another perspective, rediscovered that tradition for Anglicanism, and from it stemmed much Christian sacramental spirituality and ecclesiology.[15] In the writings of Charles Gore and those who called themselves "Liberal Catholic," the doctrine also provided a philosophical conceptuality for understanding the relation of the world to God: that through the Incarnation we are shown not only the means of our salvation but also the nature of reality itself. Thus the development of an incarnational theology along the lines of the Chalcedonian Definition has enabled some Christian theologians to challenge or accommodate new scientific and philosophical movements that appeared to threaten the reasonable foundation of Christian faith in Jesus Christ. Whatever problems it may present to us as a way of talking about the Incarnation, the Chalcedonian Definition remains a rich resource for any future attempts to explicate the belief central to Christian faith: God was in Christ, reconciling the world to himself.

The Saving Work of Christ

We have looked briefly at the way in which the New Testament writers and the Fathers reflected upon the figure of Jesus Christ. That reflection culminated in the Chalcedonian Definition, a statement that established the parameters of christological discourse in terms of a Logos doctrine of the Incarnation: the second person of the Trinity became incarnate in a genuinely human life for us and for our salvation. The Definition made the assertion in language and philosophical concepts appropriate to the fifth century, and it gave expression to the spiritual pilgrimage of Greek, patristic Christianity. In those terms it remains definitive for us today, but our continuing task is to proclaim Jesus Christ in ways that may also communicate our spiritual pilgrimage in the twentieth century.

I want to suggest a way of talking about Jesus Christ that is, I believe, faithful to the Church's tradition even though it uses concepts and images drawn from our contemporary experience of ourselves and the God who meets us in Jesus. My primary purpose will be to reflect upon our belief in him (or perhaps I should say *my* belief as it has been formed by my life as an Anglican) as an aid to the pastoral life of the Church and our proclamation of him. I do not intend to present a fully developed Christology, for I will not deal with many important aspects of the doctrine of Christ; I do, however, want to continue the development of an incarnational theology in which the Trinitarian nature of God as Father, Son, and Holy Spirit remains of paramount importance, not only as it has been received in the Church's tradition but also as it makes possible our experience of salvation in Christ. While I cannot defend the doctrine of the Trinity here, I, along with many others, believe that the neglect of the Trinitarian dimension of our redemption in Christ can only vitiate our Christology.[16] In addition, if we were to give closer attention to the indwelling of the Spirit in the Church and in the believer, we could, I think, see more clearly the unity of the person and work of Christ in salvation and sanctification, and thus rediscover some of the richness in our western and Anglican tradition.[17]

I shall examine some themes in the new Testament witness to Jesus and our experience of salvation in him, which may help us to see how our lives as Christians can be and are illuminated and made new by him through the Spirit and which may, therefore, provide us with another way of talking about who it is we believe him to be.

The Christian tradition has used many images to express what it is like to experience salvation in Christ by the power of the Spirit, and there is one significant image in the New Testament that illuminates how we come into a saving relationship with Christ by the Spirit. There shines through the accounts of Jesus in the New Testament, not only in his actions and teachings, but in his presence as a person, the sense that he is one who creates a radically new set of possibilities for those who come into contact with him and that he has the power to do so because he is able to love others without restriction. As a human being he is free to love; he can see others without fear or the need to contol or dominate. Such a quality can be, and often has been, made sentimental and trivial, but it is, in fact, a theological statement about the nature of God and the relationship of Jesus to him—a theme that receives its fullest development in the Johannine literature. Jesus' freedom to love is his power to create a new life for those he touches. In him we see one who is remembered as a person who at the very center of his being is able to be in communion with and to share in the lives of other human beings at the center of their being. He is able to judge, forgive, and heal others. He creates them anew because he is able to love absolutely. He is the man who sees others as God sees them—with love.

To speak in such a way about Jesus can be difficult for most of us (all of us, really, if we acknowledge what the Christian tradition has called original sin) because for us love is usually tied up with fear, lust, manipulation, law, pride and all those other aspects of our personality we know stand against freedom. And yet we believe that in Christ we are being transformed, made new by his Spirit, into his freedom to love others and that his freedom to love affects us at the deepest center of our lives. Such a belief can illuminate the mystery of our personhood, our being made new men and women in Christ. To explore that mystery in ourselves is also to explore why we call Jesus Lord and Savior, for the new life in Christ is one in which we see ourselves becoming our true selves, growing into the humanity of Christ (Eph 4), being formed into the image of God for which we are created and which he exemplifies.

The concept of *person* is a rich one both in the Christian tradition and in current usage. It was important to the Chalcedonian Definition (*hypostasis*),[18] and it became important for the western definition of the doctrine of the Trinity as a means of expressing the relations of God the Father, Son, and Holy Spirit. The contemporary meaning of the word is changed in many respects,[19] but there is an analogy between our notion of person and the way it was used in the theological tradition. For us, person signifies at least three qualities: the personal center of human life, the "I" out of which we act, the source of our freedom and understanding, what we call our personal identity; and it refers to those relationships through which we believe we truly become persons: the social, political, cultural, economic, and religious communities in which we come to know ourselves and without which we could not be persons. In addition, to be a person is to be one who has a history, a past, a present, and a future: I, for instance, know myself, now, as one who has come from some place, from a past I must personally acknowledge and accept if I am to grow into the completed and fulfilled person I hope to be in the future. And the same is true for the various communities of which we are a part: a community has a history transmitted through stories and symbols out of which it moves toward its future. This historical sense of person and community is of great significance for our understanding of what it is to be a person in community: one who lives from a past toward a future.

Christian faith in Jesus Christ is the belief that his historic life, which culminated on the Cross, and his resurrection and exaltation to the Father show us the depth of the mystery of being a person: one who in communion with others lives from a past toward a future. The Cross and Resurrection focus for us the significance of Jesus; the outpouring of his Spirit creates in us a new beginning and hope.

The Cross is the focus for us of the historic life of Jesus, his life as a human being, a man and a Jew. It brings together and enables us to see what there was about his life that can create new life in us and make us persons in communion with others and with God. The Cross of Jesus shows us a man who was able to give and offer himself totally for others; it shows us a man who shared in the human condition, without restriction. There are, of course, many aspects of the remembered life of Jesus which are brought together in the Cross. Three which I think especially important for the gospel tradition itself and which I believe can most clearly show how his life as a person illuminates our own are his faithfulness and obedience, his authority, and his presence as one who can judge and forgive.

Jesus was faithful to his calling, obedient to the God who led him—the God he knew at the deep level of his "Abba experience."[20] That aspect of his life spoke deeply to those who remembered him because it was rooted in the Old Testament tradition Jesus and his disciples shared. From the very beginning of its history, Israel had believed itself to be a people called to faithfulness in the Covenant God made with Abraham. The story of the Covenant is the beginning of God's call to a particular people and their response. The subsequent history of Israel was (and is) governed by the prophetic call to remember the Covenant, to be faithful to the Lord, and to live according to the Law in justice and mercy. But the faithfulness of Israel is mirrored in the faithfulness of God himself; a covenant relationship is not one-sided. Israel is called to be faithful as God is faithful in his promise to his people. The story of Israel in the Old Testament is that of a people called to believe that God would be faithful and that he would bring in his Kingdom. Nowhere, perhaps, in the Old Testament is that sense of trust in God's faithfulness and Israel's hope in his promise acknowledged more deeply than in Isaiah 40-55, in which the Suffering Servant motif dominates and in which Israel's redemption is portrayed as the continuation of God's creation of the world and his governance of all history. It is, therefore, of the greatest significance that many of the early interpretations of Jesus and of his ministry identified him with the Suffering Servant in his death on the Cross; he is the one who is faithful to God even to death, the one who offers his life as a ransom for others, and the one on whom the sins of the people are laid. In him, as the early Church came to interpret his death, God's promised Kingdom had come to pass, for he was faithful, and in him God's faithfulness is displayed. In the Epistle to the Romans, for example, Paul develops the theme that it is the faithfulness of Jesus which enables us in faith to enter into his death and to be raised to life with him; Jesus is the person in whom the faithfulness of God and the faithfulness of God's people are united to one another. The faithfulness of Jesus is also a major theme in the Epistle to the Hebrews: In his faithfulness Jesus surpasses Moses and the prophets and exemplifies the faithfulness of God (see especially chapters 3 and 12).

The faithfulness of Jesus illuminates for us the meaning of human sin and unfaithfulness. Sin is the dark side of our humanness; indeed, it is that side of us that stands against love and our becoming persons who are free to love ourselves and others. It is the lie we tell about ourselves when we try to make ourselves as gods. Only as we see ourselves in the light of the faithfulness of Jesus can we see the depth of our sinfulness. For sin is not simply breaking the law or violating a moral code— thinking of sin in that way enables us to avoid its reality by reducing it to simple wrongdoing. Sin is the denial of God for the exaltation of ourselves. In its beginning and end, sin is unfaithfulness because it is a denial of God's lordship over the creation. Sin is idolatry, hardness of heart, standing against God, living according to the flesh and not according to the Spirit; it comes from a heart turned away from God toward oneself. The sinlessness of Jesus is that in his complete sharing of our human condition he does not cease to trust in God even though he is party to our desolation and alienation from God. He is faithful in the faithfulness of God.[21] And he exemplifies the life of faithfulness neither as a demigod nor as a quasi-divine figure. In his life as a man and a Jew he shows us how a person can live for others and for God in faithfulness. Several of the Fathers clearly understood that dimension of Jesus, as is evidenced in their struggle against the various forms of Apollinarianism when they insisted that the human nature of Jesus must be one with us: "What has not been assumed cannot be restored; it is what is united with God that is saved."[22] Jesus redeems us *by his faithfulness*—in the unfaithfulness of human sin.

Jesus is also remembered in Scripture as one who speaks and acts with authority. In the Gospel he is shown as one who is able to speak out of a personal center which commands attention—"Truly, I say to you," a phrase which in the Synoptic Gospels expresses his authority and which in the Fourth Gospel expresses his relationship to the Father (e.g., John 5:19)—and also as one who is able to accomplish what he seeks to do, as happens in so many of the miracle stories. He forgives sins and brings people to a new sense of self; he can turn people from a life of sin to new life in the Kingdom. In the Sermon on the Mount and elsewhere in the Gospels he can declare who will be blessed by God. He is not just a prophet who speaks an authoritative word from God, but one who also speaks and acts from a source within himself that can interpret God and represent him in the human situation. For Paul, the authority of Jesus is most deeply shown in the Cross: Jesus has the authority to give his life for others; it is not simply taken from him. The authority of Christ is his offering of himself in the confidence of God's faithfulness and from that offering he can send his Spirit into our hearts so that we, too, can cry *Abba* and become the children and heirs of God in him (Rom 8). The faithfulness of Jesus is the source of his authority to speak and act for God as a man in the world of other men and women.

Out of his faithfulness and his authority, Jesus can judge and forgive. There is no more revelatory quality in the story of Jesus than this: He was remembered as one who can judge in love and so enable others to know forgiveness as a transforming power; he makes people new.

What we look for, and only rarely find, is a judgment in love that enables us to know forgiveness as a transforming power, one that can make us new by creating a new set of possibilities for us. We look for judgment and forgiveness that will enable us to accept ourselves in all of our weakness and sin because we know ourselves to be accepted by another, and we find such a transforming power only in those who have been able to accept themselves as loved and who can, therefore, offer love to others. To judge and to offer forgiveness as a free gift requires trust in the faithfulness of God and the personal authority of self-acceptance.

That trust and personal authority we believe we see in the life of Jesus as his story has been told to us and as he has been interpeted by those who believe in him. In the synoptic tradition of the Gospels two principal stories are told about him as one who forgives sinners. In the Gospel of Mark (2:1-12 and parallels) the forgiveness of sins is associated with the healing of a man who is a paralytic. In the Gospel of Luke (7:36-50) Jesus not only forgives a woman who was a sinner, but in the course of a parable instructs a pharisee on the nature of forgiveness: "Therefore I tell you, her sins, which are many, are forgiven, for she loved much; but he who is forgiven little, loves little." In addition there are many parables which speak of God's forgiveness freely given and his love and concern for sinners: both in action and in his teaching Jesus is shown as one who announces forgiveness. As E. Schillebeeckx points out, Jesus' very presence is the demonstration of loving forgiveness: he eats with sinners; he puts himself into the hands of sinners and shows the solidarity of God with the outcast so that

> Jesus' death becomes the seal set on a life with the conscious calling to invite sinners into fellowship: the eschatological fellowship with God, a foretaste of which may be experienced when we extend forgiveness to our fellowman (Mk 11:25; Mt 6:14-15; 18:21-35).[23]

In the Fourth Gospel, John, in his meditation on the person of Jesus, identifies him with the one who stands in judgment on the world. Jesus is the one "from above" who judges with the authority of the Father (8:21ff); he does not judge the world himself, but "he who rejects me and does not receive my sayings has a judge; the word that I have spoken will be his judge on the last day. For I have not spoken on my own authority; the Father who sent me has himself given me commandment what to say and what to speak" (12:47ff). As most New Testament scholars would now agree such sayings do not represent the actual words of Jesus, but they do convey how the community of believers had come to experience God's saving work in his word and person.[24]

In all of the New Testament interpretations of Jesus, his life as a man and a Jew culminates in the Cross: the Cross focuses for the New Testament, as it does for us, who Jesus the man was and in doing so it defines our humanity. The Cross is his final *personal* act, the completion of his life as absolutely self-giving and self-offering, the demonstration in act of his radical sharing in our human condition. He gives himself for others and in doing so shows us what it is to be a human being: a person who lives in faithfulness toward God because he knows that all that he is comes from God. The death of Christ is "not just one moral act among others. . . . It is of its nature the totality of the life of Christ in act, the definitive act of his freedom, the complete integration of his time on earth with his human eternity." The death of Christ makes possible our confession of faith that Jesus is "one nature" with us, of our being, because he shares with us completely. That radical sharing is vindicated in his resurrection in power, the event which transforms us and makes us new because it is "the manifestation of what happened in the death of Christ: the . . . handing over of the whole bodily man to the mystery of the merciful loving God, by the concentrated freedom of Christ as he disposes of his whole life and existence."[25]

There are many controversial questions about the resurrection and many ways in which those questions can be addressed. I want to consider only those aspects of the resurrection that can, I believe, help us who believe in the risen Christ enter more deeply into the mystery of the resurrection and its significance for Jesus himself and see how our life in the Church, the community of the risen Christ, enables us through the Spirit to know the power of his resurrection for ourselves.

The resurrection of Jesus Christ is not an example of universal life after death nor the intimation of our own immortality. It was precisely on this point that the proclamation of Christ crucified and raised from the dead challenged and transformed the philosophical understanding of human nature prevalent in the Greco-Roman world. Whatever else we may say about the resurrection, we must believe in it and preach it as God's creative act in the history of Jesus Christ, not as human self-achievement nor as the culmination of some divine or immortal dimension in human nature. It is an *historical* event, one which takes place in space and time and not in an ethereal or vaguely "spiritual" realm. It is not, however, an event limited to the continuum of space and time, nor is it one that can be understood through other reported instances of return from death. Thus, while there may be some continuity between the New Testament stories of the raising of Lazarus or the son of the widow of Nain, the resurrection of Jesus is not a return to the old life he knew before his death; it is a radically new life through God's creative act. As an event in our history and because it is an event which happens to Jesus who is one with us in our history, the resurrection is, in addition, an historically credible event. We cannot *prove* the resurrection as we might *prove* (to the degree we can do even that) other events in history—indeed, as the New Testament makes clear we only *prove* the resurrection by witnessing to it in the power of the Spirit—but we can investigate what happened, and such investigation can give us an indication about the historical nature of the event. That is not the same thing, of course, as believing in the risen Christ—for believing in the resurrection is faith, a gift of the Spirit—but it does mean that we can examine the New Testament testimony to the event with the reasonable confidence that we are not being simply credulous.

The stories of the empty tomb and the several appearances of Christ to his disciples and then to Paul bear witness to his resurrection in the body, and for that reason Christians confess their belief in the hope of the resurrection of the body and the life of the world to come. But we must be careful. The resurrection of Christ was not a return to his old life; it was to a new life in God. It would be wrong, therefore, simply to equate his resurrection in the body with what we know of our own bodies. In the first place the appearances themselves vary. Some are corporeal in the sense that Christ can be seen, recognized, and heard; he eats again with his disciples and they can touch him. Other appearances seem to be of a different nature and are not corporeal in the sense that we normally use that word. And even when they are corporeal, Jesus is not immediately recognized, as in the meeting on the road to Emmaus. Eyes must be opened in order that they may see and believe. What all the appearances do have in common is a quality of encounter: they are not expected and they do not occur only to those who believe. They do not fit the category of psychological visions of subjective experiences. The appearance stories point to a radically transforming event for those who saw the risen Christ; those who saw him were converted from victims of fear and desolation into witnesses and believers. In addition, when we speak of the bodily resurrection of Christ we must remember that the word "body" can have many meanings. It means for Christian people the body born of Mary, the body that dies upon the Cross and is buried, the body of the resurrection and exaltation, the body of the Church, and the body of the Eucharist. No one of these meanings or images can be taken in isolation. All of them are held together when we speak of the body of the risen Christ. For us, who suffer from a very limited understanding of "body" and usually mean by it something merely material and physical and in opposition to the spirit, holding all of the images together can be very difficult. But for Christians however difficult it may be to state, body and spirit are two dimensions of reality, not dualities in opposition to one another; human beings and events in time and space are sacramental in the sense that they are the presence of the Spirit in our space and time. The bodily resurrection of Christ, therefore, has more to say to us about our bodies and, hence, about our humanity, than our bodies have to say about his risen body. Such a consideration can, I believe, turn us in a right direction for approaching the resurrection out of our experience of the risen Christ as Savior and Lord.

In a variety of ways all of the New Testament accounts or interpretations of the resurrection associate that event with the ascension or exaltation of Jesus to the Father.[26] The account in Luke/Acts is the most explicit in terms of visual imagery: Jesus is taken up into a cloud and the disciples who are watching are told that as he has been taken into heaven so he will come again (Lk 24:50-53; Acts 1:9-11). In the Gospel of Matthew the resurrection *is* the exaltation of Jesus; in his appearance to his disciples he commissions them and tells them that all authority in heaven and earth has been given to him (28:16-20). The ending of the Gospel of Mark is disputed but some versions recount one appearance of Jesus and say that he was taken up into heaven and took his seat at the right hand of the Father (16:9-20). In the Gospel of John the crucifixion itself is the exaltation of Jesus (8:28; 12:32). The accounts of the resurrection appearances say nothing about his departure, but John has Jesus speak of the Counselor whom he will send when he goes away (16:5-7) and of his being glorified in his death as he was glorified before the world was made (17:1-5). The Pauline Epistles do not speak of a visible ascension, but they do see the resurrection as Jesus' reigning in power in the new age (e.g., Romans 1:1-6; cf. 1 Corinthians 15:20-28; Ephesians 4:7-10; Philippians 2:9).[27] The Epistle to the Hebrews develops an explicit theology of the exaltation of Christ: he has entered into heaven itself to appear in the presence of God on our behalf (Heb 9:24).

In all the New Testament stories of the resurrection and exaltation of Jesus there is a confession of faith in him as one who now is with God and whose life and death have been vindicated by God. The resurrection/exaltation is for Jesus a new life and a new creation; for those who believe, it shows the unity of Jesus with God; it is the confirmation of his life from the beginning. In whatever way that confession of faith may be formulated (that is, in the image of the Apostles' and Nicene Creeds where Jesus is "seated at the right hand of the Father" or through the more conceptual language of the Chalcedonian Definition), it is fundamental to our belief about Jesus:

> As in the incarnation we have to think of God the Son becoming man without ceasing to be transcendent God, so in his ascension we have to think of Christ as ascending above all space and time without ceasing to be man or without any diminishment of his physical, historical existence.... In the incarnation we have the meeting of man and God in man's place, but in the ascension we have the meeting of man and God in God's place, but through the Spirit these are not separated from one another.[28]

The unity of Jesus with God is the hope of our calling in him, that is, our salvation, our unity with God in Christ, and our sharing in the divine life. There are dimensions of the remembered life of Jesus that can show us something of what the unity of Jesus with God might mean for us, in that they illuminate our humanity, our being as persons. Through them we can see Jesus, able and willing to offer himself for others in the radical self-giving of the Cross, culminating a life that demonstrated the freedom of love. Because the resurrection and the exaltation enable us to confess in faith that the human life of Jesus is now centered in God, we can also confess him as the one who shows us the hope of our calling as human beings: to be centered in

God through him who shared our human nature. And he does that not by ceasing to be human but by becoming what it is to be truly human: one whose human life is fulfilled in the triune life of God. At the same time, however, we do not know what the phrase "union with God" means; we use it only as the expression of our hope. For us the unity of Jesus with God can only be approached from our side of his resurrection and exaltation, and for that reason we say in the creeds of the Church that "we believe in the Holy Spirit . . . we look for the resurrection of the dead and the life of the world to come" (the Nicene Creed) and "I believe in the Holy Spirit . . . the resurrection of the body, and the life everlasting" (the Apostles' Creed). Our hope is possible through the Spirit in the community of belief, the Church. In other words, Jesus shows us what it is to be truly human; but, if that were all, his life would be only an example to us, one which we could emulate and admire—a form of adoptionism. The final word of faith about Jesus Christ is that he makes us new and creates for all of us the hope and possibility that in him we can be centered in God through the gift of his Spirit. In the Church we have a communion with one another and with Jesus Christ that enables us to become persons, to grow by grace into our eschatological hope of union with God in Christ, and to witness to others the saving power we have known.

The experience of salvation in Christ by the Spirit makes it possible for us to confess about Jesus what the Christian tradition has claimed and stated in many different ways: that he is the Logos of God, the eternal Son, the Second Person of the Trinity, of one being with the Father. He can, in other words, offer us the gift of the Spirit which makes us sons and daughters of God because he himself shares in the life of God by nature; he is "God with us," the instrument of creation in whom all things were created and through whom all things are being made new. The crucifixion and the resurrection and exaltation reveal who Jesus is and enable us by faith to believe that what was experienced in the presence of Jesus of Nazareth and what we in every generation experience in him is eternally true about him and about his significance for all human beings. To live in Christ by baptism into his death is to be indwelt by his Spirit and to have his continuing presence as the hope of our calling (Rom 6:3-11), as the pledge of our inheritance (Eph 1:14), and as the power of the New Creation, transforming Christian people and, we believe, all who do not yet know his name and presence, into the image of God. In the Eucharist of the Pentecost community our humanity now is with God in Christ and we are being transformed into the power of the new life in him by the Spirit which he gives us.

4

The People of Grace

Richard A. Norris, Jr.

The purpose of this essay is to sketch an approach to a theological understanding of the Church and its ministry. This is a fairly modest aim—and rightly so, since the problems of ecclesiology are complex and numerous and do not readily lend themselves to brief or summary treatment.

In the contemporary world, for Christians as well as for nonbelievers, the very notion of "Church" has become difficult to understand. The problem is that traditional language about the Church does not quite fit—does not work well—when used in reference to the relatively novel phenomenon called "denomination." A national or multinational religious corporation is simply not the sort of thing the term *ekklesia* is designed to describe, and this circumstance is a source of frustration to theologians, who keep talking about Church in terms that do not comfortably mesh with any observable social reality, and to ecumenists, whose efforts to bring about "Church union" serve only to strengthen the very type of organization that is one of the sources of their problem. The inevitable result of this situation is that theological talk about the Church is out of tune with people's (including theologians') experience. This, though, may not be a bad thing, for it means that such talk functions, whether intentionally or not, as criticism of the social shape of the Chris-

tian movement in the contemporary world. In present circumstances, any thoughtful ecclesiology automatically becomes an
effort to get Christians to see their common life differently.

The most obvious and basic reason for this state of affairs is
the development frequently referred to as the "privatization of
religion." Coeval with, and not unrelated to, the emergence of
the denomination has been the appearance of a culture—a
shared way of seeing, valuing, and asking about things—that has
no place in the public reality it defines for religious categories of
explanation. Under these conditions, religious faith becomes
perforce an individual and purely personal matter. This means
not only that it becomes a matter of individual option or decision, but also—and more important for our purposes— that the
realm in which religious language functions, and in which it
applies, is that of the private and interior life of the individual.
Obviously, this state of affairs has an effect on perceptions of
religious groupings generally, and of the Church in particular.
The religious community is seen as a by-product—an external,
social objectification of the private needs or ideas of discrete
individuals, set up and maintained by such persons to serve
their ends. An organization or institution of this sort, however,
can scarcely be regarded as a proper subject for *theological*
discourse. It does not, after all, fall within that interior and
personal realm which is the only sphere where talk about God
makes sense. On the contrary, it belongs to the exterior object-
world of secular reality. In this way, Church becomes the name of
something external to the life of faith.

The effects of such attitudes in the life of the Christian
community are manifold, if often unnoticed. The "religious
institution" (as it is called) is normally envisaged as instrumental—as an "aid" to the individual, as a service organization or a
corporation dispensing a religious "product." Its officials are
seen less often as leaders in their communities than they are seen
(and therefore behave) as managers, salespersons, advocates, or
"professionals" in the provision of certain sorts of service. At the
root of all such tendencies, however, lies the fundamental problem of the divorce between the interior and personal life of
religion and the external world of social reality. It is this divorce,
firmly rooted in the modern consciousness, that any theological

discusssion of the Church must address; for what the word "Church" connotes above all is a social reality which is itself the sphere and the from of a certain relation to God—a "people" whose ordinary social and historical existence is understandable only in terms of grace. The problem is to see why and how this is so, and what it implies about the order and mission of such a people.

I

We start off, then, perhaps naively, by inquiring what the Church is "about"—what issue or problem or reality its existence answers to and what affirmation is made by its presence in human history. In other words, we begin by raising a question about the *horizon*, the reference point from which the Church is located and understood, the basis or foundation of its existence. Such an inquiry, however, inevitably leads us back to the Church's origins, to the circumstances in and out of which this human grouping arose.

It is no doubt true that Jesus of Nazareth did little or nothing in the way of founding an organized society to perpetuate his ideas or his work. To put the matter bluntly, the *ekklesia* does not have Jesus as its designer. Nevertehless, it is true that the Church owes its existence to what Jesus did and taught and—above all—to what became of him, to his dying and resurrection. For this reason, any search for the Church's horizon must begin with Jesus himself and with that band of disciples that became the seed of the later Church. To ask what Church is "about" is to ask what Jesus' ministry, death, and resurrection are about.

Fortunately, it is not difficult to identify the issue addressed by Jesus' ministry, the issue that gave significance to his death and his triumph. If there is one thing that stands out in the pages of the Gospels (even if we grant the difficulties of using them as modern-style historical narratives), it is that the theme of Jesus' preaching and teaching, of everything that he did or stood for, was the *basileia tou theou*: the "rule" or "reign" or "kingship" of God. His ministry presented itself as a promise, a warning, and a foretaste of a new state of affairs in which the Creator would finally make the world of human choice, action, and struggle one in which God's loving purpose for humanity is supreme. The reign of God, then, meant the overcoming of humanity's alienation from God in sin, and hence a transformation of human existence in which "The kingdoms of the world" should "become the kingdom of our Lord and of his Christ" (Rev 11:15).

The horizon, then of Jesus' ministry—the issue or reality in the light of which its significance appears—was this coming redemptive reality, this salvation, symbolized by the phrase "reign of God," a reality that Jesus characterized both as the one thing worth having and as a reversal and overturning of the established and sinful order of things that prevailed in the world he knew. His ministry did not set out to create or establish this reign of God, but to announce, signify, and presage what God was bringing about. To this end he gathered disciples and associated them with himself in the task of signifying God's reign. In particular he assembled that mysterious Twelve, whose very number was symbolic of Israel, the people that belongs to God. He assigned them a role as heralds and servants of the *basileia tou theou.* "They went out and preached that men should repent. And they cast out many demons, and anointed with oil many that were sick and healed them" (Mk 6:12-13).

If in these Twelve (and in the larger circle which they represented) we are to acknowledge the seed, the beginning, of what was later to become the Church, then we already have, in principle, an answer to our fundamental question. What we have called the Church's "horizon"—the reality in the light of which it exists and understands itself—is no different from the horizon of Jesus' own ministry. It is nothing less than God's rule, that coming fulfillment of all things which is, at the same time, God's judgment on what the world has made of itself in its alienation from him. The Twelve, both in their constitution and in their activities, point to a world redeemed, to the coming transformation of things under God's fulfilled sovereignty. The people that belongs to God—the people the Twelve symbolize and inaugurate—is thus a people that stands for the new order of God's rule.

Here, though, we must take another step. If the Church

stands for the rule of God, it does so in a way that is, in one crucial respect, different from the way the Twelve originally stood for it. The difference is made by what happened in the end to Jesus himself. For the fulfillment of Jesus' ministry—the fulfillment of the promise it embodied—came in his death and resurrection. It came, that is, in a way that attested the "beyondness" of the new order in relation to the present age (for the Cross only affirms this age in the act of negating it), and at the same time pointed to Jesus himself as the one in whom the new order already exists—as the one in whom God is with humanity and humanity is for God. The resurrection of Jesus, with the outpouring of the Holy Spirit that accompanied it, was experienced as the dawning of the age of promise, and in this experience Jesus himself was acknowledged as the one in whom and for whom the reign of God is real. From that moment forward, then, to point to the coming redemption, to point to the *basileia tou theou*, meant to bear witness to the risen Christ, "the beginning, the first-born from the dead," in whom "all the fullness of God was pleased to dwell" (Col 1:18-19).

Thus, the Church, the continuation in a new mode of the body of Jesus' disciples, signified God's reign as Jesus himself did. The horizon of its existence is indeed the same as that of his ministry. The only difference is that by virtue of his death and triumph, he is himself now merged with that horizon. For the Church, God's sovereign rule is all tied up, one might say, in the Christ, and it is by standing in with him that people touch and taste the power of the love of God and can thus look forward to the transformation of human life and its world which Jesus' ministry meant and intended. The Church, in other words, stands for the reign of God by standing for Christ. After the experience of the resurrection, the two cannot be separated.

II

Here, then is at least a preliminary answer to our question about this people called "Church": it is a body of disciples— learners and followers. What it follows is Jesus, but Jesus acknowledged as the risen Christ, the one in whom the promise of God's new creation is realized and who is thus its "horizon," the reality in the light of which, and with reference to which, it exists. No doubt such an account of the Church falls far short of being complete, but it does establish some paths along which further inquiry can proceed.

To begin with, we can inquire into the meaning of the image of a "body of disciples." Clearly the term "disciple" refers to a transitional status. A disciple is one who is in the process of becoming something but has not yet achieved that goal. The Church, accordingly, is to be understood as a body which does, indeed, stand for something and intend it but does not fully embody what it stands for. It is still "on the way" and on pilgrimage, pointed toward and focused on the life its teacher represents but not measuring up to it at any point. And clearly enough, this is a fair description of the Church as people know it. It stands for and aims at a life which, nevertheless, it only manifests in a relatively feeble, intermittent way.

Yet disciples, whatever their shortcomings, are never apart form their master. The condition of being a disciple is contingent on the presence of the master and, indeed, on a sharing of life with the master. This means that the very existence of a body of disciples depends on the willingness of the master to take them on, to be patient with faults and longsuffering where weakness and backsliding are concerned. Here, too, there is a parable of that body of disciples, followers of Jesus as the Risen One in whom humanity has been fulfilled in God.

The point of our figure is no doubt fairly plain, but it will do no harm to spell out some of its implications. In the first place, it conveys an essential truth about the very basis and shape of the Church's existence. This body of disciples, as we have called it, is not constituted primarily by its profession of, or its loyalty to, a set of rules or ideas or ideals. On the contrary, it is constituted through a living relationship to the one who is its teacher because he is also its horizon, the embodiment of what it stands for and seeks. All discipleship entails concrete involvement with the life it seeks to imitate and share. It presupposes that the disciple is taken on by, and indeed taken into, that life. As a body of disciples, then, the Church depends for its very existence on a power that transcends it—something "beyond" that offers itself and confers its presence. The Church exists—and exists solely—in virtue of the grace by which it is involved with the Christ for whom it stands and intends.

What this grace effects, and what such involvement amounts to is limned for us not only in the pages of the New Testament, but in the whole record of Church experience and tradition. In the first place, to pursue the language of our parable, there is the matter of being "taken on." The society of disciples exists because, before anything else, it is "taken on" by God in Christ, and this in spite of faults, perversities, and rebellions. The basis of discipleship, in short, is the divine initiative in forgiveness. The body of disciples is an assemblage of forgiven—justified—sinners. They are people who in repentance have accepted the judgment passed on them by God's new creation in Christ and in this way have come, by faith, to acknowledge that their life is in Christ: "hid," as St. Paul says, "with Christ in God" (Col 3:3).

With this phraseology, however, we are introduced to a second aspect of the grace that establishes the community of disciples. The disciple is not only taken on, but "taken into" the life of the new creation, the human future Christ embodies. In the New Testament, this work of grace is especially associated with the gift of the Holy Spirit. Through the Spirit's activity the power and life of God's fulfilled reign are communicated to believers in the form of a "down payment," a foretaste. In this way the logic, shape, or rhythm of the new life in Christ is shared with believers, and they can be said truly to enter into his way of being and to bear, if only in a preliminary and immature way, the identity of the one into whom they are called to "grow up" (Eph 4:15). It is this relationship that is meant when the Church is said to be, through the operation of the Spirit, Christ's "body," an extension, as it were, of who and what he is. To be an assemblage of disciples is to have "received Christ Jesus the Lord" and so to "live in him, rooted and built up in him" (Col 2:6f).

It is no mistake, then, that his people, this body of disciples—which once was "no people" but now is "God's people" because it has "received mercy" (1 Pt 2:10)—should be described as "the people of grace." The many-sided significance of that description must, however, be stressed. It means, to begin with, that what founds the Church or grounds it is precisely a relationship to God in Christ through the Holy Spirit, a relationship brought about, therefore, not by human aspiration, conviction, or contrivance but wrought by God himself. To be sure, human response is of moment in this relationship—else why speak of a "body of disciples"? Nevertheless, such response always, at every point, has God's initiative as its precondition. It becomes possible and meaningful only in a situation created by grace. Discipleship, then, subsists in the medium of grace. The identity of the Church—the fact that it is the assembly of those "sanctified in Christ Jesus" (1 Cor 1:2)—depends at every moment on its being sustained through the Spirit in the life of that coming reign of God which Christ represents and embodies.

To describe the Church as "people of grace" means that discipleship is a pilgrimage in which human nature is pointed toward its own elevation, to a way of being that at one and the same time transcends and fulfills its present capacities. The expression "people of grace" does indeed, as we have said, imply the gratuity of the relationship that grounds the Church's existence. At the same time, it points to the "cure" of sin—the forgiveness which overcomes alienation—as an essential moment in this relationship. More than either of these, however, it implies that humanity under grace is "ek-static," self-transcending, for grace is creative of fellowship with God, the Ultimate who exceeds the limits and forms of creaturely existence. Thus, the oft-repeated tag to the effect that "Grace does not abolish nature but completes it" is true as long as the completion in question is not taken to mean mere "finishing off," but a fulfillment in which humanity is opened up to a new dimension of possibility—the possibility of being with God in Christ. As Irenaeus of Lyon once put it:

> This, then, is the order and such are the rhythms and the guidance by which the humanity which was (originally) made and fashioned comes to be in the image and likeness of the ungenerate God. The Father determines and commands, the Son executes and performs, and the Spirit nourishes and gives growth, while humanity bit by bit makes progress and

rises up towards fulfillment—that is, comes to be close to the Uncreated. For only the Uncreated is fullness, and this is God. So humanity had first of all to come into being, and once created, to grow; and having grown, to achieve maturity; and having matured, to be multiplied; and having been multiplied, to become strong; and having become strong, to be glorified; and having been glorified, to see God; for it is God who is to be seen, and the vision of God brings incorruptibility with it, "and incorruptibility makes one close to God."

(AH 4.38.3.)

With this evocation by Irenaeus of the theme of God's Kingdom, the time has come to turn to a second line of inquiry. We have been exploring what is implied or presupposed in the picture of the Church as a body of disciples under grace. But what are the implications of the other half of our initial proposal—of the statement that what Christian discipleship intends and stands for is God's *basileia*, his reign in Christ? In this connection, there is one central and essential point to be developed. God's *basileia*, the new creation in Christ, signifies a state that can only be called "the world," the creation of God as a whole. It refers, in other words, to what St. Paul had in mind when he spoke of "the creation itself," obtaining "the glorious liberty of the children of God" (Rom 8:21), or to what the writer of Ephesians pointed to when he spoke of a "fullness of time" when "all things" would be summed up "in Christ" (1:10). What the people of God stands for and intends, then, in virtue of its relationship under grace to God in Christ is not just a redeemed body of disciples, but a redeemed world.

The importance of this point can scarcely be stressed too strongly. It suggests first of all that the future, the "beyond," with which the Church is involved through grace is anything but an un-worldly or an anti-worldly reality. On the contrary, it is the world itself as it will be when God is "all in all" (1 Cor 15:28). To put the same point in another way, the Church in intending God's fulfilled reign intends its world; the horizon of discipleship is a transformed human, and therefore natural, order. Christian doctrine, indeed, hints at this truth when it insists that the first thing to be affirmed about the natural and human world is not its sin, corruption, or alienation, but the fact that it is

God's creation, and, therefore, a reality which is intrinsically *for God*. From this it follows, however, that the Church itself is quite properly a phenomenon in and of the world—whose redemption in Christ it intends. It is a human society whose life is intricately woven into the contingencies of history, a segment of the creation itself. No doubt the Church is, at the same time, set apart in its world by having a distinct social identity, but that is in order that its discipleship may point the world to its destiny "in Christ."

It is not and cannot be, then, a matter of chance, coincidence, or contrivance that the Church is a people, a social reality. If what its discipleship intends and symbolizes is God's creation liberated, reconciled, and restored in Christ, then its own way of being must be commensurate with what it seeks and "means"; that is, it must exist, act, and speak as a complex whole, a human society rooted in the natural order and composed of interdependent parts, a world in miniature. Some such conclusion is demanded by the way in which the Christ himself, the Church's horizon and identity, is portrayed in the New Testament. There as we have often enough heard, Christ is presented not as a mere individual, but as a "corporate personality"—as the Second Adam in whom the human race even now lives virtually, and who, in turn, wills to dwell in the body of his disciples. It is not, therefore, the individual believer who in the first instance bears the name and identity of Christ, but the Church (1 Cor 12:12). The Son of Man is an individual no doubt, but an individual whose identity is socially actualized; and it is the Church—a society—which is the "one new man" that is created in Christ (Eph 2:15). The Church is a social reality because in meaning and intending the Christ, it means and intends not just an individual but a new humanity.

Hence, if we ask what discipleship it is that intends, shares, and, thus, intimates the new creation Christ is, our answer must be quite straightforward: it is that of the people of God, the Church in its collective and communal identity. It is in this people, and, therefore, *in relation to others*, that the individual believer becomes a "christ," an anointed one, and so a bearer of the meaning of the new life in Christ. Consequently, the people, the social reality called "Church," is not a secondary objectification of individual needs, values, and beliefs or an organization that exists to serve them. From the point of view of any particular believer it is rather the presupposition and matrix of the life in Christ; and insofar as that life "beyond" can be intimated and manifested by a human, here-and-now reality, it is the Church as a complex network of different, various, yet interdependent individuals that alone can come close to representation of the whole Christ, the Second Adam. What stands for, intends, and symbolizes God's world transformed in Christ is the discipleship of a visible society.

This, however, brings us back to our starting point, to the matter of discipleship and its conditions. To say "Church" is not to say "club," "corporation," "party," or "organization"; it is to say "people"—a *visible social body* composed of all sorts, ages, and conditions. What constitutes this people, what marks it out and makes it, from a human point of view, recognizable, is the fact that it professedly aims at, intends, and stands for a transcendent reality—God's new creation in Christ—the definitive historical manifestation of which was the ministry of Jesus, which it proclaims to be the proper horizon not only of its own but also of the world's life. As such, it is an assemblage of disciples—persons who, whatever their other characteristics and varying degrees of understanding and commitment, want to stand with Christ and to grow in the new life he embodies. At this same human level, therefore, the Church means and stands for something: God's world transformed and redeemed in Christ.

None of this, however, makes, or can make, any sense at all unless the transcendent life which the Church seeks is present; unless it is "in Christ" as God's people through the gift of the Spirit. There is a dimension of the Church's life which cannot be captured in any account that refers only to human factors. If "Church" exists at all, it exists because the depth and ground of its life, that which makes its stumbling discipleship possible, is the gracious presence, through the Spirit, of the Christ whom it intends and follows. If it proclaims Christ, that can only be because it receives Christ. If it intends God's fulfilled reign, that can only be because it is touched and moved by the power of the new creation it seeks— by the Spirit of God. "Church," then, is a word which refers to a mystery in the proper sense: a perceptible and—at one level—entirely explicable phenomenon which nevertheless is involved with, and, therefore, intimates and coveys something beyond itself.

That "beyond," however, that identity of the Church "in Christ," is not something the people create or control: it is a gift—grace. The Church does not dispense it, but lives in it and by it, and in its power practices a discipleship by which God's fulfilled reign is flickeringly manifested in the life of the world. The grace of God in Christ, then, is both the ground and the significance of the Church's life: its ground, because apart from that grace, the Church is an organized fraud, speaking of what it does not know, and its significance, because what grace conveys is a participation in the world's horizon, the new creation in Christ.

What this adds up to is that in speaking of the Church, one must practice a strange combination of caution and boldness. On the one hand, if one intends to speak seriously of "Church," it is necessary to speak, in the strictest sense, *theo*-logically, referring this society at every point to God and God's work in Christ. On the other hand, it will not do to identify the Church as simply a "divine institution"—absorbing, as it were, the people's transcendent horizon into its historical life. To speak of the Church is always to speak of a body of disciples—not so much knowers as learners—whose way of being is to discount itself in favor of what it intends and proclaims. If the Church can claim anything for itself, it is not any moral perfection, nor yet any a priori cognitive certitude, but the presence with it, in its teacher, of the God whose reign it "means." Perhaps, then, those theologians are correct who have suggested that the Church is best conceived as a living sacrament, a body whose discipleship means—and presupposes—the real presence of the Christ it intends.

III

The Church is a people that bears and heralds the new creation in Christ. It is a school of disciples that is also, under grace, a community of forgiven sinners and a body rooted by the

Spirit in the life of Christ. That it is a *people* whose life has this shape and sense means that the Church takes social form in human history and that it sustains and actualizes its identity through social institutions. The church has an *order* of some sort through which it knows and becomes what it is.

"Order," or course, is a word of complex meaning. To the modern ear it connotes "organization" and some sort of structure of power. There can be no doubt that the Church, in every era of its history, has indeed been organized, whether formally or informally. Simply to identify order with organization, however, is to risk missing the point of talk about "church order," for in modern parlance, "organization" signifies primarily the rational ordering of means to ends, whereas order, in the case of the Church, has to do above all with the question of *identity*, that is, with the structures through which a society *is what it is*. Understood in this sense, the order of a society (and its structure) is prior to its organization. It operates not at the level of constitutions, but of institutions.

In order to clarify this point, something must be said about the meaning of the word "institution" as we are using it here. By "institution" is meant a recurrent, patterned practice or form of action which, for some particular purpose and in some specifiable context, enacts the logic and basis of a community's way of life. This definition excludes many phenomena as institutions. In America, for example, Thanksgiving dinner is an institution, just as, for the members of certain clubs, playing a game of bridge may function as an institution. In the life of the Church, too, one can discern a plethora of significant institutions, from going to Sunday School and making novenas, to revival meetings and retreats. Each of these phenomena is a shared, patterned form of behavior by which a society is maintained and rooted in its way of life.

No matter how many such phenomena can be detected in the Church, though, there are certain institutions that count as central and definitive for its life. These are the events or activities that occupy its normal gatherings as a whole people, and they can be observed to have done so throughout its history. One thinks, for example, of the reading, meditation, and exposition of the Scriptures; of Baptism; of confession of faith; and of celebration of the Eucharist. Each of these activities explicitly occupies itself, in one way or another, with the Church's relation to the horizon which constitutes it—that is, with the mystery of people's relation to God in Christ. Each is a normative common *leitourgia*, public office, of the people of God; hence, each is an institution which *orders* the Church in the proper sense, giving the Church its identity.

This means that in the Church these liturgies must be understood in two ways at once. On the one hand, they can and must be understood simply by analogy to similar institutions in other human groupings. They function as vehicles of the community's identity through time. To enter into them is to repeat an action which bears a certain meaning and which, for just that reason, grounds the present community in the tradition its institutions carry. Such practices are perfectly ordinary social instruments of communal identity and continuity. We have seen that the Church's communal identity is constituted by its relation to a reality that transcends it, the new creation in Christ, and which it knows and experiences only through grace. Accordingly, the institutions which carry and sustain the Church's identity as a human community in history are at the same time the vehicles of its relation to God in Christ. As actions in which the community intends the source of its life, they are media of the grace by which it lives. Like the Church itself, these institutions have a sacramental character; they "order" the Church on the social and historical plane in the very act of referring and relating the Church to its "beyond"—to God in Christ.

In what precise way, though, are these institutions or liturgies related to what is ordinarily referred to as the "order" of the Church? And what is the significance of the fact that institution and order are in fact closely bound together? Before answers to these questions can be suggested, three preliminary considerations must be noted.

First of all, it is necessary to stress the importance and centrality of these institutions in the life of the Christian people. Its existence and theirs are correlative. On the one hand, the Church perennially comes to be, is actualized in and through these institutions. Should they cease, the body of people called "Church" would cease to assemble or to act *as Church*. On the other hand, these institutions mean what they mean and effect what they effect only as institution in and of the Church. Except in the presence of the Church, the books of the Bible are not Scripture. Apart from certain actions of the Church, bread and wine do not mean the Body and Blood of Christ. There is the closest possible relation between these liturgies and what we have called the identity of the Church; the two depend upon each other.

But it must be stressed that order is the matrix of authority in any community—or, in other words, authority resides fundamentally in those factors in a community's life upon which its identity is seen to rest. No person, pattern of behavior, or way of speaking is authoritative absolutely, that is, in and of itself. It acquires authority only within a society or community, and only insofar as it stands for, embodies, or expresses that which is seen to make the community what it is. Power can be defined and limited at the level of organization, but what legitimates power is authority rooted at the more fundamental level of what we have called institutions. Hence, the "order," the structure of authority, of a community (and a fortiori of the Christian community) has its foundation in the institutions through which that community's identity is established and maintained.

Finally, it is important to note that what we have called "institutions" in the life of the Church are, in fact, complex events. For one thing, they are composite actions, involving steps taken over a period of time. Furthermore, the carrying out of these actions involves not merely acts or gestures but also the words which convey their meaning—forms of prayer or thanksgiving or confession, for example. (In the case of the exposition of the Scriptures in preaching, words constitute the act.) Again, these institutions entail the use of things: water, bread and wine, a book, a table, to name only the most obvious. Finally, and not insignificantly, human actors are involved in these events— leaders and participants, who speak words, make gestures, and handle things. All these elements or factors in the event or institution are, moreover, closely interrelated; the identity of the community is actualized through the mutual interaction not only of the human participants but also of conventional words and physical objects.

There is a structure implicit in the institutions or liturgies through which the people of God knows and constitutes itself as just *that* people; and the point to be made here is that this structure is diffused through, and so reflected in, the wider life of the Church—in its general order. Consider, for instance, the conventional verbal forms which figure in the Church's institutionalized public actions. These forms continue to function outside such liturgies, where they regularly serve as points of reference for the community's teaching and self-understanding. The most obvious, though by no means the sole, example of this phenomenon is the baptismal confession of faith, which grew and developed in the setting of the institution of baptism, and which, as "creed," has become a focal basis of catechesis and reflective theological construction. Or consider the Scriptures themselves. Their very definition as a "canon" sprang in part out of a need to specify which Christian books should qualify to be read in the people's regular liturgical assembly. Their status as an authoritative list and a norm has to do with their function as media of the horizon which assigns the Church its identity. In connection with this role, the Scriptures have always functioned beyond the setting of the Church's primary institutions. They become the matter of personal meditation and appropriation on the part of individuals, as well as of interpretation for doctrinal and moral purposes. In this way they become a structural factor in the whole spectrum of the Church's life. The persons who habitually take a role as leaders in the communal liturgies become its officials and representatives in a variety of other spheres: in governance, in teaching, and even in administration. In this way the Church's central institutions, its public liturgies, embody and focus the media of its identity, and, thus, the structures of authority which serve to guarantee its identity in all other areas of its life.

It must be stressed that this "order," which is embodied in or springs out of the Church's primary institutions, is a structure at once complex and balanced. The authority which governs the Church at the deep level of order is not vested in any single factor in its life. To be sure, the persons who are its official leaders are endowed with authority, but their authority depends upon their being answerable to the other bearers of the tradition in which the people's identity is declared, most notably to Scripture and creed. For their part, Scripture and creed are interdependent because each declares the meaning of the other. Yet neither speaks at all save as it is made to do so by the ministry of readers, expositors, and preachers—a ministry focused in the leadership of the congregation. To put the matter summarily, authority and order are resident primarily in a total structure, not in any single element within it. In that sense, they are quintessentially communal.

But let it not be forgotten that the identity this structure or order maintains is an identity conferred from the Church's "beyond," an identity whose foundation is grace. The Church's order, therefore, is indeed immanent in the communtiy, but what that order means and conveys is the Church's transcendent horizon—its life in Christ. For this reason, like the institutions or liturgies in which they primarily function, every factor in the Church's immanent order is in practice set apart within the Church as a symbol and a medium of grace. The Scriptures, human works though they are and humanly used, are marked out as "Word of God" and "revelation" because they convey to the Church the Christ who is its life. The consecrated elements of the Eucharist are treated as holy things because of the reality, the Christ-life, which they mean and convey. The Church's liturgical confessions of faith, too, are vehicles of the relationship with God in Christ which grace creates. Finally, when the Church solemnly ordains a human being with prayer and the laying on of hands, it sets that person apart *within the Church* as a symbol and minister of the same grace which the Scriptures proclaim, the sacrament enacts, and confession of faith appropriates. The interdependent elements of, or factors in, the Church's order share the quality of the institutions in which they primarily function. They are the ways through which the people of God refers itself to the grace by which it lives.

With this much said by way of preface about the "order" of the Church, it is possible and reasonable to turn more particularly to the subject traditionally closest to the hearts of Anglicans: the ministry of word and sacrament as that is focused in the person of bishop, priest, or deacon. But on this subject, too, some general and preliminary considerations must be registered by way of evoking the sense or point of the expression "ministry of word and sacrament."

To begin with, it must be clear that when people use this expression they are referring to a matter which has to do with the *order* of the Church and not primarily with its organization. Organization, we have suggested, is concerned with the rational adjustment of means to ends, of resources to goals. It is a socially formed answer to the question, "How shall we go about getting *A*, *B*, or *C* done?" Order, on the other hand, answers the more fundamental question, "Who or what is the 'we' that wants to set about this task?" The question of order, in other words, is precisely the question of the structures that maintan a community's identity. There can be no doubt that the Church is and, to one degree or another, always has been organized; that ministers of word and sacrament have tended to figure prominently in its organization; and that order and organization feed into one another. Nevertheless, the two questions can be distinguished— indeed, no sense can be made of the ministry of word and sacrament unless they are distinguished—for word and sacrament concern not the organization of the Church but its being and identity.

In the second place, the phrase "ministry of word and sacrament" says something about the role of the ordained ministry in the ordering of the Church. First and most obviously, it specifies the function of that ministry at the level of order, which is, quite narrowly, to be in the service of the preaching of the Word and the administration of the sacraments. More than this, though, it calls attention to the fact that the ordained ministry is one, and only one, element in the basic structure of the Church's order. To say this, of course, is to do no more than reiterate in another form what has already been said: that the fundamental media of the Church's identity are its characteristic institutions or liturgies, and that what is called "the ministry" represents just one of the several interrelated factors which figure in the occurrence or performance of these institutions. The ordained ministry serves and guarantees the identity of the Church only as it ministers to the message which is the burden of the Scriptures and to the life—the life in Christ—which the sacraments, with the Scriptures, communicate. It is the organic complex of ministry, word, and sacrament that orders the Church and is the effective sign of its identity and continuity.

Finally, in using the expression "ministry of word and sacrament," we are deliberately reducing to a level of secondary importance the question of the precise shape and nomenclature of that ministry. Anglicans have frequently maintained that the so-called "threefold ministry" of bishops, presbyters, and deacons is (a) a matter of apostolic institution and (b) essential for that reason to the very existence of the Church as Church. Of these two propositions, the first can be shown, on historical grounds, to be almost certainly false. The threefold ministry appeared and prevailed in the course of the second century and not before. The most that can be said about it is that it has come to represent the typical and normal shape of the ordained ministry in almost all times and in almost all Christian bodies. This is in itself significant, for it means that as a matter of *fact* the order of the Church has been generally tied into the traditional office of the chief pastor with a body of associates or delegates on the one hand, and a body of assistants on the other. Nevertheless, this circumstance does not justify the second of our propositions. The threefold ministry is not a priori and of necessity the sole legitimate shape of an ecclesial ministry. What is a priori and of necessity, and what can reasonably be shown never to have been lacking in the Church in one form or another, is precisely a ministry of word and sacrament; hence, we shall discuss the normal, and in practice normative, form of that ministry under this more general rubric, for our aim is not to deal with the form of the ministry but with its status and function.

For our purposes, the important and obvious thing to be noticed and understood about this ministry is simply that it is "set apart," consecrated, by solemn acts of ordination in such a way that the person so ordained retains this status, this relation to the community, for life. In modern times, such a setting apart has seemed offensive to some because it creates distinctions, and even a certain kind of rank among Christians. Ordination brings with it standing, leadership, and authority in the community— not exclusive, to be sure, but real and automatic. Why is this so?

There are many answers which might be given. One might,

for example, point out that persons who occupy official or unofficial leadership roles are a necessity, or at any rate a reality, in every sort of human community. Such an answer, however, does not touch the question of Church order—the question, that is, of what the office of bishop or presbyter or deacon has to do with the identity of the Church at the institutional level. To deal with this question it is necessary to reiterate what has already been said both about the nature of the Church's institutions and about the various elements or factors involved in their "happening." These institutions have what can only be called a sacramental function. They are ordinary instruments of communal identity and continuity, but they are at the same time media of the transcendent horizon that defines the identity of the Church. The setting apart of a ministry of word and sacrament is more than an acknowledgment that the Church, like any other social grouping, is bound to have its leaders and office-holders. More important, it is a way of saying that the primary leaders and office-holders of the Church shall be persons whose primary role is, as ministers of word and sacrament, to mean and symbolize the grace which is the ultimate ground of the people's existence. Bishop, presbyter, and deacon are "set apart" in order that they may *as persons* mean to the Church its identity in Christ. Such a relationship to the Church *as a person* does not cease with a given term of years.

Such "set apart" persons are a ministry *in and of the Church*— not above it or outside it—because what they "mean" in their functional role is the identity which belongs communally to the Church. On the other hand, their ministry is *set apart* within the Church to mark the fact that this identity does not belong to the Church immanently, in its own right, but comes to it from its defining "beyond." Their ministry is a signification of the Church to itself; and they carry this ministry out primarily and focally in the Church's definitive liturgies.

This signification of the Church to itself, which accounts for the status of ordained ministers as sacramental persons, cannot be confined by their roles in the community's primary institutions. It quite naturally broadens to encompass more general pastoral roles—now, however, shared at every point with other believers, who are in their own right bearers of the communal identity which the ordained ministry signifies to the Church. And there is little that can be said to define or delimit what this extended ministry may entail. If one wanted to specify in very general terms what the character of such pastoral ministry is, the answer could only indicate its fundamental aim rather than the particular activities it might involve. The overall aim of a ministry whose calling is to signify to the Church its transcendent identity in Christ can only be the nourishing of the community in discipleship—the business, that is, of growing into Christ in the various callings, responsibilities, and circumstances of human life. The order of the Church—and of the ministry, which is but one element in its fundamental structure—exists to ground the life of discipleship.

IV

As we turn to the question of what the Church *does*, its role or function, as distinct from the question of its order, we will see that discipleship remains central to our discussion. It must be conceded that in contemporary discussions of this issue, "mission" is a term more popular than "discipleship" for denoting the characteristic business of the Church—perhaps because it carries a connotation of purposeful dynamism on the part of people who, as the phrase goes, "have something to give." There are, however, good reasons why "discipleship" may be the more useful term to employ.

One reason is that "discipleship" is more inclusive. It embraces the full range of human concerns and activities. To be a disciple of Christ is not to be engaged in some narrowly specific kind of activity; it is to be engaged in conforming one's life in all its dimensions to a certain pattern, to a certain hope. The importance of this consideration, moreover, becomes obvious when one contemplates the character of the Church as a social group. Whatever organizational shape it has taken under the suasions of its environment, from feudal fiefdom to modern corporations, the community always remains, as a whole, stubbornly unspecialized. It is not a party seeking exercise of political power, a company selling a product, or a pressure group oriented to one or more definable causes. It is a *people*, and for just that reason its concerns and activities extend to every area of human existence, including education and health, spirituality and politics, art, and the conduct of personal relations. To be sure, there are within the Church subgroups both specialized in their interests and aims and organized to achieve them. In itself, this circumstance is just further evidence of the variety and breadth of the concerns that figure in the following of Christ. The only category which can convey the shape or logic of such variety is that of discipleship. The Church's engagements and activities may be—indeed, are— many and many-sided, but in all of them the community is about the business of growing in and enacting its identity in Christ. That is its fundamental calling.

There is still another reason why the category of discipleship is useful and central in understanding the Church's "doing." Better than any other word, "discipleship" conveys the preliminary and tentative character of the Church's actualizations of its identity. Living by grace, and, therefore, with the need as well as the assurance of forgiveness, the community of believers has no accomplishment not subject to repentance as well as rejoicing, to criticism as well as affirmation. Since the Church is a parable and a sacrament of God's new creation in Christ, what its activities achieve is not that horizon itself but portents and anticipations of it, whether in the goodness of an individual life, in an exalted moment of common worship, or in an act of making space for justice in its social world. To speak too blandly and bluntly of "the Church's mission" or its "ministry to the world" may suggest that there is some final fulfillment Christian action might confer or achieve; to speak of discipleship is to acknowledge that in all its members the Church has learning and growing to do *in* its working.

Finally, there is this to be said about the category of discipleship: the designation does not run the risk of inducing people to think in exclusively instrumental terms about the Church and its institutions. One of the striking characteristics of a great deal of contemporary talk about the Church, especially, perhaps, in North America, is that it works almost instinctively with a rationalizing means-ends calculus. This is entirely understandable, since Christians as well as others are prone to envisage the community of believers almost exclusively on the model of a modern organization, that is, a grouping whose fundamental *raison d'être* is the marshalling of powers and resources to a definable end or ends. The first thing, after all, that one asks of any group trying to increase the efficiency and success of its operation is the question of ends. "What is your product?" "What is your goal?" There is good sense in such questions; but where the Church or its constituent groupings are concerned there is also risk—the risk that the community itself, its members, and their common life will become one-dimensional: so many functions, as it were, to be understood solely in terms of service to external ends. No doubt the Church has work to do, but its primary work is the realization in Christ of a truly human way of being for the world—discipleship, work in which the doers and the deed are not related as means and end. The Church is not instrumental to something other than its own realized identity.

What is involved in discipleship? What goes on when the Church enacts or actualizes the identity in Christ which grace confers upon it? To speak in the most general and ideal terms, the life of discipleship embraces two essential and inseparable dimensions. There is, first of all, the spiritual and moral growth of its individual members, and second, there is the social shape of its common life as a people. These go hand in hand. The spiritual and moral awareness of individuals contributes to the making of a certain sort of community, while the hopes and values embodied in a communal life shape, in their turn, individual habits and perceptions. In both cases the aim of discipleship is the same. It is to enter into and reflect the new life of God's reign in Christ, to enter into Christ's relation to God on the one hand and to humans persons on the other. As St. Basil of Caesarea insisted centuries ago in his Monastic Rules, Christian existence is guided by the double commandment of love to God and to neighbor—a commandment in Christ that is not so much an injunction as a fulfilled reality into whose spirit we are lifted by grace.

Such simplicities are in the end no simple matter. To enter into and share the life of Christ in this sense is to turn away from attitudes prevailing in "this world" and, through "renewal of your mind," to be "transformed" (Rom 12:2); hence, discipleship involves criticism and challenge both of the values of the world and of the structures of conviction and power by which these values are maintained. Since believers themselves, as products of their world, share these values and are shaped by these structures, it also involves a dialectic of self-criticism. Thus, discipleship in one way or another inevitably enters upon the way of the Cross—the way Jesus followed when he became a "sign of contradiction" in his time and place. The Church, in its following of Christ, will stand under the sign of the Cross, for its way of being will question the idolatries and the injustices of the world in which it is set. To love God above all things is to reject the ultimates the world creates for itself, and to love one's neighbor in God is to refuse to acquiese in the injustices the world visits on those to whom it is indifferent or whom it despises and fears.

The matter, however, cannot be concluded quite so simply. The death of Christ does indeed mark the world's rejection of God's love as Jesus' ministry embodied it; it signifies that in the world the body of Jesus' disciples will represent, as he did, a "sign of contradiction." As every honest preacher knows, the Church means and stands for something that does not *fit* in the prevailing system of things—sometimes in a formal way (that is, by virtue of the truth its institutions carry), and sometimes in a genuinely material and practical way. Yet the Church is neither apart from this world nor hostile to it. On the contrary, it is the worldly *sign* of the world's transformation in Christ. What it hopes and intends for itself, therefore, it inevitably hopes and intends for the world. The community of believers knows that the Cross does not mean God's repudiation of the world to which his Word was sent in Jesus but, rather, that in the light of the resurrection, the Cross becomes a symbol of the world's redemption—its coming reconciliation to God. The death of Jesus is the worldly event that points to that new creation. Even as a sign of contradiction the ministry of Jesus, as fulfilled in his death, was a ministry *for* the world. Accordingly, the Church's discipleship affirms the world, the world which God creates and redeems, even as it challenges and criticizes it. It does this simply because it *is* the world—world practising discipleship. It affirms its world because what discipleship intends is world-transformed-in-Christ.

In and of itself, discipleship involves mission—witness and service for the world. It is an active signification and seeking of the world's redemption. It proclaims, announces, and points to what the ministry of Jesus intended, and that is not the Church itself, but the fullness of human life in God. This witness, intrinsic to the practice of discipleship, is not limited to some one aspect of, or moment in the Church's life. Denominations may be prudent to have central bureaus of "mission"; but witness is not a "department" of Christian existence in the world. It takes every form the activity of the Church itself assumes.

The Church proclaims the new creation in Christ as gospel. It does this by word—by preaching. It also carries out proclamation by manifesting a way of life that lends substance to its word—by example. The aim of such proclamation is not to fill the Church's buildings, but to open people's eyes to the good things God has in store for them. No doubt those who hear what is proclaimed and so understand themselves and their world "in Christ" will be reckoned among God's people. What the proclamation has in mind, however, is not the multiplication of Church members, but "Christ in you, the hope of glory" (Col 1:27). That Pauline phrase does indeed make a good summary of what the Church has to say.

"Saying," however, is not the only, nor even, in all circumstances, the principal mode in which the Church bears witness to God's reign in Christ. Jesus preached, but he also healed, cast out demons, and brought people hope in the circumstances of their daily lives. Words, after all, require deeds to embody them, for what the word says, the deed makes real—just as the word interprets what the deed accomplishes. Inevitably, the Church's discipleship and witness take the form of what can be called "making a difference in the world." The people of God, by virtue of its discipleship, is in the business first of *showing* signs of the new creation in Christ and then of discerning and *acknowledging* such signs when, by the providence of God, they occur through secular agencies and apart from its own witness. That is, discipleship both creates and calls attention to circumstances in the life of the world that "mean" God's new creation because they speak of his presence and activity in the Spirit. And since, by hypothesis, such signs are not private affairs, performed in secret for a few, but open and public signs, whose medium is the world itself, to create or acknowledge them is perforce to alter the shape of life in human society. Such activity may take the form of charity and service, from the care of the sick and the homeless to the creation of new hope for those the world has shut out. It may also—and indeed, historically speaking, invariably has—taken the form of action to alter social and political circumstance; and this social witness of the Church is as much a part of its discipleship as are proclamation and service. Indeed, it is inseparable from them. Serious proclamation and devoted service cannot create signs of God's reign without making social and political "space" for them in the world; and they soon enough extend themselves into the task of shaping the world to make that space.

No doubt all such witness is flawed—as is all Christian proclamation and service. The Church does not cease to need or to live by God's forgiveness, even when it is about the business of practicing discipleship and doing good works. Repentance, after all, is the logic of its life, the means by which it becomes both a sign of contradiction in a world that refuses repentance, and the bearer of a new hope. Repentance is not, at its heart, a matter of negation; it is a matter of positive choice. It comes to people who hear good news, discover themselves in Christ, and want to celebrate God's "new thing." It expresses itself both in a constant willingness to grow and change and in a desire to dress the world up for its glorious destiny. And that is how—as a body of disciples which by grace shares in the new life of Christ—the Church lives.

5

The Structure of Christian Community

Louis Weil

The underlying root of the word 'structure' comes from a Latin verb meaning 'to build.' The use of this word in the title of an essay on sacraments suggests a very specific approach to the fundamental questions of sacramental theology, an approach which perceives the sacraments in terms of dynamic energy, a building up of the Body of Christ.

Our customary use of the word 'structure' in English can be associated easily with a static, virtually unchanging reality. A great structure, an important architectural monument, is admired precisely because its unchanging character reminds us of an earlier age, an age whose remaining monuments are a tangible link with a past time. There have been various attempts in the evolution of sacramental teaching to approach the meaning of the sacraments in this latter sense, to see them as divinely instituted and precisely defined sacred realities which offer the Church an unchanging unity with the sacramental worship of every previous age.

It is only possible to construct such a sacramental theology if one is either wonderfully naive or uninformed about history, for from the very beginning, there has been significant evolution in every aspect of the Church's sacramental practice. Neither the relation of the sacraments to the authority of Christ nor their significance as a sign of the unity of the Church throughout every age rests upon a static and unchanging sacramental faith and practice. The dependence of the sacraments upon the authority of Christ and their power as instruments of unity rests, rather, upon the organic relation between Christ and the Church.

Our word 'construct' offers us a more appropriate access to the meaning of the word 'structure' in this essay. 'Construct' suggests action, an active doing, a building up. If we use 'structure' as a verb, we see this underlying sense: 'to structure' means to integrate the constituent parts of a whole according to their inherent mutual relations. Such an integration, in turn, manifests the special and distinctive nature or character of the whole. This definition offers us a penetrating insight into the nature of sacraments as structuring the constituent dimensions of the Church as an integrated whole. Baptism thus *creates* the Church: it structures the diverse human reality into a single body. It is, according to St. Thomas Aquinas, "the door of the sacraments" because it establishes the fundamental groundplan of unity in faith formed through the integration of the diverse members.[1] So it is that baptism establishes the sacramental context in which all other Christian practice unfolds, and through which the unity of the body is built up.

Such an approach to the role of the sacraments finds its source in the teaching of St. Paul. The coinherence of the lives of the various members of the Church is compared by Paul to the diverse parts of a human body which, taken all together, constitute the one body. In the Epistle to the Romans, the comparison is made in these words: "For as in one body we have many members, and all the members do not have the same function, so we, though many, are one body in Christ, and individually members one of another" (12:4-5). This emphasis upon the unity of the body is stated even more urgently by Paul in the Epistle to the Ephesians, where he calls for a lifestyle characterized by "lowliness and meekness, with patience, forbearing one another in love, eager to maintain the unity of the Spirit in the bond of peace." The source of such a transformed lifestyle, Paul continues, is the one God whose essential unity characterizes the whole Christian revelation: "There is one body and one Spirit, just as you were called to the one hope that belongs to your call, one Lord, one faith, one baptism, one God and Father of us all, who is above all and through all and in all" (4:3-6).

Paul's reference to the one baptism is linked to the unity of the body in his first Epistle to the Corinthians where the comparison of the Church to a body finds a rich expression:

> For just as the body is one and has many members, and all the members of the body, though many, are one body, so it is with Christ. For by one Spirit we were all baptized into one body—Jews or Greeks, slaves or free—and all were made to drink of one Spirit. For the body does not consist of one member but of many ... Now you are the body of Christ and individually members of it. (12:12-14,27)

Paul's discussion of the unity of the body with such explicit reference to baptism indicates the crucial importance of baptism for each member of the body as an act of incorporation into the unity of the Church. Paul's theology of the unity of all the members of the body depends upon a common physical and sacramental act by which that unity is signified. This link is also made in reference to the Eucharist in another passage of the same epistle where Paul sees the sharing of the bread and cup as constituting, that is, both expressing and building up, the unity of the body: "The cup of blessing which we bless, is it not a participation in the blood of Christ? The bread which we break, is it not a participation in the body of Christ? Because there is one bread, we who are many are one body, for we all partake of the one bread" (10:16-17).

In this teaching of Paul we find the essential idea of the sacraments as building up or structuring the life of the Church. They are dynamic acts which take place regularly within the community and give form or shape to the corporate experience of the gift of faith in Jesus Christ. Faith thus has a primacy over sacramental acts.

Sacraments and Faith

The sacraments presume faith and are articulations of it. Without faith, the sacraments are merely an external ritual without internal meaning. Faith is corporate; it is God's gift to the Church, which itself comes into existence in human history through the generative love of God revealed in Jesus Christ. The Church is the visible community of those who recognize and trust this Incarnation-presence of God and whose members have been incorporated into this self-disclosure of God through baptism. It is around this self-disclosure of God in Christ that the life of the Church is structured. The members of the Church are both nutured by this presence and are also the agents of its proclamation to the world. Through faith the believer is given access to an intimate union with God—sharing in the divine energy which enlivens and nourishes the whole body. Faith is given sacramental articulation through incorporation in baptism, and this unity is in turn signified and deepened through the common eucharistic meal. Without faith, the sacraments are like a body without breath or blood.

It is astonishing to note how seldom studies in sacramental theology speak about the role of faith in relation to the sacraments, yet from their genesis sacramental actions are expressions of faith. As physical creatures, it is through our bodies that our internal dispositions are communicated. To use but one example, love is not a matter merely of interior ideas nor of words alone; the full expression of love involves the whole human person. And so it is also with faith. As our response to God's creative and redemptive love, faith requres an enfleshing, a response in which our whole physical being participates. This is the principle upon which the whole idea of sacramentality rests, and it is a necessary complement to an incarnational faith. In the words of Tertullian, "The flesh is the hinge of salvation."[2] The outward, physical aspects of a sacrament are, in this perspective, the instrumental means by which faith is expressed. A sacrament thus embodies both God's gift of grace and the human response of faith.

The continuity of the response of faith through sacrament is exemplified in an especially powerful way by the Eucharist. We have come to think of the Eucharist as a liturgical act quite clearly detached from baptism in regard to fundamental meaning. The Church's sacramental practice for several centuries after the resurrection of Jesus is a helpful correction to this error. Eucharist was seen as an integral aspect of the process of Christian Initiation, and was itself the culminating act of incorporation. The gathering of all the baptized on the first day of each week to celebrate the Eucharist was nothing less than a recapitulation of the meaning of the whole process of incorporation into Christ's body. The celebration of the Lord's death and resurrection—the paschal feast—recalled the community to its fundamental unity in Christ established through baptism. This same approach is found among Anglican writers of the seventeenth and early eighteenth centuries who see the gathering of the Church for Eucharist as the primary sign of the baptismal covenant.[3] It is in the Eucharist, then, that faith is expressed, but at the same time nurtured and renewed. Faith always involves this extension of commitment throughout the whole of life. Although there is an intensity of meaning focused in a particular sacramental act, as, for example, when a person is born anew through the waters of baptism and made a member of the Body of Christ, nevertheless, the full meaning of that act is a life-embracing event. What is signified and effected in the sacrament grows to an ever deeper maturity in the ongoing life of faith, or else it shrivels and dies.[4]

The ongoing life of faith is not an individual or private religious concern. It was said earlier that faith is corporate. This is proclaimed in a particularly effective way in the practice of infant baptism. The baptism of an infant cannot be an expression of the faith of an individual who is at that point incapable of such a faith-response. Infant baptism speaks pointedly of two aspects of every sacramental act: it signifies God's gift of redemptive love by his own initiative toward us in our helplessness, and it also signifies the corporate nature of faith since it is because of the Church's faith represented in the gathered community that the infant is brought to the waters of baptism at all. Because of their faith, that of the parents, the Godparents, and the local community, the Church incorporates the infant into its common life where God's gifts to it will be nurtured by the ministry of mature believers.

Yet these two dimensions are constitutive of every sacramental act. Every sacramental act is first of all an expression of God's reaching out, of God's initiative, and the context of our response is always shaped by the corporate faith of the Church. This is no less true at the baptism of an adult than of an infant. The adult is generally capable of some expression of personal faith, but that is not an independent gift to the individual. The personal faith of an adult is also nurtured and matured within the framework of the common life. Even after many years of committed, mature Christian life, we continue to find that our personal faith is affirmed and strengthened by the faithful lives of other members of the Church. God's covenant is with all the baptized as members of an organic whole, a people who share a common faith and celebrate a common identity in Christ, whose life-giving death they proclaim in every sacramental act. Without that faith, the sacraments are no more than a ritual façade.

With such faith, the sacraments effectively signify the meaning and purpose for which they exist in the Church; they become the instruments of grace, signs of the divine energy by which God touches and transforms the lives of believers. Grace is nothing less than God's gift of self to human beings. Christian belief in the Incarnation establishes a principle by which we discern the signs of this divine gift in the whole range of human life. God's grace is not limited to the sacraments, but the sacramental principle enables us to recognize God's presence and activity beyond the framework of liturgical rites, so that we are permitted to see the Christian sacramental system as rooted in what are the universal elements of our common humanity. To suggest that God's grace is effective only through the sacramental form is to be propelled quickly to the threshold of magic; God is not bound by our forms and rituals. But to recognize in the ecclesial sacraments the sign of God's way of self-giving to the whole created order is to discover their purpose in the building up of the unity of the body. In this perspective, the sacraments cannot be a private means of grace since they always unite us to the whole family of faith in a common offering of praise and thanksgiving. In spite of their essentially corporate nature, however, the history of the Church reveals a gradual privatization of religious experience and a consequent loss of a sense of the corporate foundations of faith, sacrament, and grace.

Initiation and the Christian Life

For the past several centuries, the manner in which baptism has been celebrated and the theology which has developed alongside it, have contributed to the shaping of a deeply distorted understanding of the meaning of Christian Initiation and its relation to living the Christian life. The rites of the *Book of Common Prayer* (1979) hold up a restored model of the corporate dimensions of baptism, but the confusion and antagonism, not to mention indifference in some places, which have greeted the new rite are indicative that ritual changes alone will fail unless they are rooted in a restored image of the Church. In other words, there must be a penetration of the meaning or concept of the Church upon which the new rite is based, or we are left with only a surface approach to issues which lie well beneath that surface.

In the mind of a significant number of Episcopalians, both laity and clergy, baptism is seen as an essentially encapsulated event, a private matter somehow related to individual salvation, but not as the sacramental ground plan of the Church's corporate life. In spite of the new *Book of Common Prayer,* baptism continues to be celeberated at least semiprivately, both for adults as well as children, because an individual's baptism is not really seen as a concern for the parish community. Parents with little or no Christian commitment in their own lives continue to bring their infants for baptism because *their* parents demand it. This is possible and is not seen as an act of hypocrisy primarily because baptism is understood as an end in itself and not as the beginning of a way of life. It is a brief ritual unrelated to the wider framework of the Church's life. It can continue to be understood in this way because this is how baptism has been experienced for innumerable generations, and that experience has shaped a folk theology of individual salvation. For many, baptism has become a religious commodity, to be obtained much as one might drop into a store on infrequent occasions to pick up rarely needed supplies.

A few years ago I presented a program on Christian Initiation to a gathering of laity. My primary concern that day was to emphasize the relation of baptism to the whole range of the church's ministry: evangelization, ongoing education, pre-baptismal instruction, the corporate celebration of the rite, and the extension of baptism in the ongoing eucharistic life. After I had set forth this comprehensive view, I asked for questions and responses. I immediately found myself confronted by an angry vestryman who said, "It sounds to me that you are like a Fuller Brush salesman who opens up his display and says, 'You cannot buy only one brush. You must buy them all'." This anecdote offers an excellent example of the understanding of the sacraments, and of baptism in particular, which has developed over recent centuries and which the new rites attempt to correct.

Two fundamental problems are reflected in the vestryman's reaction. First, he saw no essential relation between baptism and the wider dimensions of ministry. It was, so to speak, a separable act which could be detached from the continuing signs of Christian faith. In an ironic way, it was unconnected to the Church. The occasion of such a baptism, he felt, might establish goodwill in the parents, and this in turn might lead to some future commitment. Given the appalling statistics of defection from any continuing practice of Christianity after baptism by such indiscriminate standards, the hope for such a positive commitment is naive at best. Baptism is a sign: it signifies incorporation into the community which lives by faith in the death and resurrection of Jesus. If baptism is detached from that signification because of the Church's failure to make the essential connections, the sign will in the end be left with no substantial meaning. That is, to be honest, the present situation in many parts of the Church.

The second problem in the vestryman's comment derives from the first. A disconnected baptism is no longer perceived as a dynamic action which continues to shape day-to-day life. It becomes static, an objective structure rather than an act which itself structures or shapes the experience of Christian faith. As we have seen, this leaves us with sacraments understood as commodities, sacred objects which may or may not attract one's interest and concern; rather than being bloodstream, life sustainer, and renewer of the body, they are more like the appendix, a vestige of what was once a living organ.

A deepened understanding of baptism, an understanding which emphasizes its connectedness to every aspect of the Christian life, gives added meaning to the assertion of Aquinas that baptism is "the door of the sacraments." If it is baptism that establishes the sacramental framework of Christian experience, as was suggested earlier, then there must be inherent and fundamental connections between baptism and all other sacramental acts. We have already suggested the existence of such an essential connection between baptism and Eucharist. Yet it is equally appropriate to speak of any sacaramental act subsequent to baptism as an articulation of the relation already established by baptism between God and the community of faith.

Two sacraments traditionally known in the Anglican tradition as *lesser* sacraments gain in significance when we consider them in their relation to the baptismal mystery. These two sacraments are confirmation and penance. Anglicans are familiar with the idea of a relation between confirmation and baptism, with confirmation understood either as a complement to or completion of a previously celebrated baptism. The link between penance and baptism is probably less evident to Anglicans. In the context of this discussion of Christian Initiation it is useful to restate the relation of both confirmation and penance to a renewed understanding of baptism.

Anglicanism today has inherited a certain ambivalence about the meaning of confirmation in spite of its firm rooting in Anglican practice. In the Episcopal Church in America, confirmation has been especially valued as a sign of Anglican identity and of the pastoral/sacramental ministry of the bishops. The ambivalence about confirmation stems from its history long before the Reformation, when it emerged as a distinct episcopal rite from the complex of rites forming the initiatory process. The early pattern of initiation, of which we have far greater knowledge today than was available even a century ago, manifested an essential unity which encompassed a diversity of elements. This essential unity spoke clearly of the sacramental nature of the Church itself. For the first several centuries candidates for initiation passed through a succession of rites, which shaped a process of Christian formation and incorporation.

A distinct rite of confirmation developed historically as bishops became separated, for a variety of reasons, from the majority of celebrations of the water rite, the latter coming to be generally delegated to the parish priests. Confirmation emerged as an expression of the bishop's essential connection with the rites of initiation even when it was not possible for him to be present for the water rite, and was, at first, to be performed as soon as possible after the baptism. Practical matters led eventually to a significant delay of confirmation and consequently to a loss of a sense of its relation to the water rite. It became a separate sacrament, and in that process began to develop a theology of its own, distinct from the water rite.[5]

The English Church was heir to this medieval situation at the time of the Reformation. Archbishop Thomas Cranmer (1489–1556) was influenced by Protestant sacramental teaching from the Continent and thus centered the entire meaning of Christian Initiation around the water rite. Into that dominical rite he assimilated much of the meaning of medieval confirmation through the placing of a prayer with a signing of the cross on the forehead immediately after the water rite. His preservation of a distinct rite of episcopal confirmation as a later complement to the practice of infant baptism left the Anglican tradition with a potentially ambivalent situation: Is confirmation to be understood in its medieval sense as a detached element of the initiatory rite, or rather, in what seems to have been Cranmer's intention, as a rite at which a mature profession of faith by persons baptized in infancy is solemnized by a laying on of hands by the bishop? The *American Book of Common Prayer* (1979) recognizes this ambivalence in our tradition but, on the basis of much recent scholarship,[6] gives primary weight to the latter interpretation. With either approach, however, it is obvious that the meaning and pastoral significance of confirmation are derived from its relation to baptism.

An affirmation of the connection of penance with baptism does not bear the burden of so complex an historical background because any relation between the two has seldom received significant comment in Anglican teaching. Penance has been seen either as an element in corporate worship or in private spiritual discipline as a part of preparation for the reception of communion. Yet if the classical Anglican teaching that the gathering of the Church each Sunday to celebrate the Eucharist is itself the constantly renewed sign of the baptismal covenant, then penance as a preparation for eucharistic communion finds its primary significance as the restoration of our baptismal identity. Sin is not merely a private matter. Any sin against God in whom the baptized share a common faith is at the same time a sin against all the members of the Body of Christ. The reconciliation absolution effects after we have acknowledged sin is an ecclesial reconciliation; it is a restoration of individual penitents to the integrity of that unity which is formed through the one baptism. Penance is not, then, a matter of optional personal piety. It is an essential sign of the baptismal life in which sin is acknowledged and forgiven so that we may continue to live without hypocrisy the promises we have made in the baptismal covenant.

Liturgy as Ecclesial Act

The primary meaning of all sacraments is found in the *being* of the Church: the sacraments are public acts which manifest the nature of the Church as the primordial sacrament of Jesus Christ. The history of the shift from sacramental action to an excessive objectification involves a long evolution in liturgical piety which lies beyond the scope of this essay.[7] The issue touches, however, on the more fundamental ecclesial question which has manifested a renewed significance in the thinking of many contemporary theologians. The particular sacraments draw their sacramentality from the prior and all-embracing sacramentality inhering in the Church as the body of Christ. It was on this basis, that, in the nineteenth century, the leaders of the Oxford Movement thought of the sacraments as the "extension of the Incarnation."[8] They are abiding signs of the presence and ministry of the incarnate Lord for and in the life of the Church which is his body. In a very particular way—through the mode of sacrament or outward sign—they fulfill the Lord's promise to the Church: "I am with you always, to the close of the age" (Mt 28:20).

This ecclesial nature of the sacraments, that is, their rooting in the corporate faith of the Church, has been progressively obscured over the course of several centuries. The early concept was that a sacrament is an act of the whole baptized community. If it had been asked, "Who is the celebrant?" the only possible answer would have been, "the Church," for it is the whole Church which was understood to celebrate its unity of faith in

Christ in the sacramental rites. This ecclesial or corporate concept depended upon the community's self-consciousness as the body of Christ, for through baptism they had entered into the most intimate identification with the Lord. Indeed, in the end, it was Christ who was understood to preside over every sacramental rite because he was present in the gathered Church, for "where two or three are gathered in my name, there am I in the midst of them" (Mt 18:20).

For a variety of reasons, this ecclesial sense of the sacramental act gradually gave way, under the influence of social and political as well as theological factors, to a very different attitude in which ordained clergy are viewed as the primary agents in sacramental acts. Parallel to the emergence of this clerical authority over the sacraments there developed, inevitably, a complementary diminution of the role of the laity. Sacramental rites became the privileged and protected domain of the clergy, who celebrated the sacred actions for the benefit of the laity rather than in union with them. The result is that for many centuries the liturgy has been viewed as the domain of the clergy. Although this situation had reached an extreme by the late Middle Ages, it must be admitted that the Reformation was not very effective in addressing the problem and restoring an integrated participation. Although the Reformers saw the problem, the general state of lay education militated against a reversal of the pre-Reformation situation, and liturgical authority continued very much under the exclusive control of the ordained clergy.

The reason for raising the issue of clericalism is not to denigrate the clergy, nor to underestimate the importance of their role in the life of the Church. Rather, we need to link clericalism to the understanding of the Church of which it is a symptom. Clericalism is not the fault only of the ordained, for many laity are content to conceive their role in the Church in primarily passive terms as recipients of the spiritual goods supplied to them by the clergy. Although ordination certainly is an authorization for appropriate liturgical leadership, the distortion of this legitimate role through an authoritarian clericalism produces a caricature of ecclesial liturgy. The norms of liturgical practice are a mirror of the Church since liturgy is an act of the

Church's self-realization. A style of celebration in which the priest usurps most other roles and in which the participation of the laity is primarily passive, somewhat as spectators, offers us a clericalized model of the Church in which ministry is conceived essentially as the work of the ordained.

Much of recent liturgical reform has moved in the direction of a sane declericalization, but the transition out of clericalism can be very difficult. It requires the emergence of new patterns of parish worship in which laity with appropriate formation are involved both in planning and in celebration. The simple efficiency of the clerical models makes it all too easy to expect the clergy to provide the rites according to an essentially professional model. Certainly the responsible leadership of the priest is an important aspect of the whole process, but the integral involvement of the laity in both planning and participatory roles permits the community to claim the liturgical celebration as its own and to experience it as a truly corporate offering of praise and thanksgiving. If such an ecclesial model is to be permitted to emerge, it will require significant changes in the patterns of seminary liturgical formation which we have inherited from the past. Future priests need to look closely at the clericalized model which was often the pattern of their own parochial experience. If a clericalized mentality persists in our seminaries, and if the implications of an ecclesial mentality are non enunciated and examined—as well as experienced—it is likely that many candidates will perpetuate an authoritarian clerical model after ordination.

The Formative Impact of Ritual Practices

We have suggested that the liturgy is a kind of image of the Church; as the Church's self-realization, the liturgy manifests experientially the operative model of ecclesial identity. It is thus possible to look at liturgical practices, to examine and evaluate them, asking if the model of the Church implied in a particular practice does signify the understanding of the Church we find in the New Testament model, namely, a fellowship of believers.

Such an evaluation of liturgical practices is not as easy as it might seem because we have not generally looked at such customs from this perspective. Liturgical practices also seem to have a life of their own, and often both laity and clergy become deeply committed to various gestures and rituals whose meaning and development are quite unknown to them. Once such customs have taken hold, any criticism or proposed elimination of them seems to strike at the heart of the experience of those for whom the particular gesture has acquired an unquestioned importance in the expression of their faith.

One familiar example of this phenomenon was the custom in many Episcopal churches of a genuflection at the phrase "and was incarnate of the Virgin Mary," in the recitation of the Nicene Creed. This genuflection was not authorized by the rubrics of the Prayer Book tradition, but had come to be superimposed upon Anglican practice in those parishes which were influenced by Roman Catholic liturgical customs. During the course of the Vatican II reforms, the practice was removed from the Roman rite as part of a process of simplification which led to the elimination of liturgial customs introduced, for the most part, during the late medieval period of ritual elaboration.[9] When some Anglicans suggested that, for the sake of consistency, customs borrowed from Rome which had never been authorized in the Anglican Prayer Book tradition should be terminated, a not uncommon rejoinder was the curious idea that the removal of the genuflection was an indication of an abandonment of belief in the Incarnation on the part of Anglicans.

This is, of course, a rather minor example of what is in fact a far more serious issue in regard to sacramental theology and practice. The theology of the sacraments is not a set of pure ideas detached from earthly, physical consideration. Quite the opposite. As we have suggested, sacramental rites are explicit articulations of the sacramental principle that God uses the physical realities of this world as instruments of his presence and grace. Sacraments can never be separated from their human, physical, material celebration. With regard to the sacraments, theology and practice are placed in the most intimate union possible by an incarnation in which the grace of God is instrumentally signified through the external, physical form.

Given this perspective, it is inevitable that ritual forms will incorporate a variety of liturgical customs accruing to the sign at first almost unconsciously—often when a priest adds a gesture for a first time to a phrase which seems spontaneously to compel this outward expression. This is probably the way in which the whole range of liturgical gestures, especially those associated with the proclamation of the Eucharistic Prayer, were introduced into common liturgical practice. What originates as a spontaneous gesture is then taken up by others to whom it seems appropriate, and thus the gesture, a sign of the cross for example, enters into the general liturgical pattern.

There are, of course, many such ritual patterns preserved in the various liturgical families of the Church. Anyone who has ever attended a celebration of the Byzantine rite in an Eastern Orthodox Church recognizes immediately the difference of ethos reflected in the pattern of liturgical gestures employed by the bishop or priest who presides at the liturgy. Most Orthodox laity, and perhaps many of the clergy, are probably unaware that the basic aspects of this ceremonial pattern are secular in origin, having been taken from Byzantine court ceremonial of the fifth and later centuries. For Orthodox believers, this ritual pattern is an integral aspect of their nurture in the sacramental life of the Church, and suggestions for needed reforms, for the removal of levels of ritual encrustation, are generally met with strong opposition. The reason for this is that the liturgy is, in a very profound and often unconscious way, a formative experience. It communicates the grace of God to the faith community, but that communication takes place through external forms which have been shaped under the influence of cultural, social, and, often, political factors. Once assimilated into the liturgical tradition, the forms become a fundamental dimension of the sacramental experience itself.

It is precisely the subtlety of this formative aspect of the liturgical experience which makes an urgent demand upon the Church to look at its inherited pattern of ritual practice and to ask if the signs are shaping an ecclesial consciousness which conforms to our best insights into the nature of the Church as the body of Christ. The ultimate problem with over-clericalized liturgical models is that they manifest *and form* a clericalized understanding of the Church's nature. Such an understanding must be placed under the judgment of the model of the Church which we see reflected in the New Testament, in which we find clear examples of leadership and ministry in the body, but not a narrowly clerical authority.[10] A celebration of the Eucharist in which the priest, for whatever excuse, usurps the diverse ministries of the community is the expression of a theology of the Church whose concept of ministry will inevitably focus upon the liturgical ministry of the ordained clergy.

Liturgical Ministry and Pastoral Oversight

The role of the ordained priest as the celebrant of the Eucharist offers the most fruitful context for the consideration of these matters. The connection between ordination to the priesthood and authority to celebrate the Eucharist is an assumed fact in the sacramental Christian traditions. It is a connection, however, about which there has been inadequate reflection, and it is taken for granted that it is simply ordination which gives this authority or power. Certainly designation for ministerial office in ordination includes responsibility for the sacraments, but there is a danger here of being sensitive to only one aspect of the issue. If this view is stated in the extreme, the ordained priesthood would seem to be independent of the ecclesial community, which priests are ordained to serve. The ordained priesthood could be interpreted as somehow standing apart from or against the laity, and we may find examples of such a view maintained in the past.

The other aspect of ordination, an aspect which in no way diminishes the importance of the laying on of hands by a bishop as the sign of the continuity of ministerial authority, is the ecclesial dimension, the constitutive role of the wider Church, the laity, in the calling forth of the ordained ministries of bishop, priest, and deacon. Ordination is not an act which involves only the clergy, although certainly the manner in which many ordinations are celebrated seems to imply just that. Rather, ordination is an ecclesial act, and as we have said with regard to the sacraments in general, Holy Orders is a sacrament explicitly built upon the reality established through baptism. The sacramentality of Holy Orders is a derived sacramentality, dependent upon the fundamental and all-embracing sacramental nature of the Church. Ordination is not a narrowly clerical act; it is an ecclesial act in which the ordained bishop has a particular ministry to perform. It is the whole Church which ordains.

This is a fundamental theological assertion if we are to avoid a mechanical concept of priesthood in which one priest can be equated with or substituted for another priest in regard to sacramental power, rather like a sacrament machine whose ministry can be isolated from the question of personal faith and common membership in the body of Christ. For the first several hundred years of Church history there was a firm sense of the role of the local community in the raising up of persons who would be ordained through and for that community.

Clergy and laity are not autonomous states in the Church. They are never independent of each other, and neither can alone constitute a local church. Their ministries are complementary within the one fellowship of the baptized, the Church. The ministries of the ordained clergy have meaning only through their rootedness in the community of faith. Although it is the bishop who imposes hands in ordination, and thus gives witness to the source of all vocation in the purposes of God, at the same time the bishop stands within the Church, is a minister of the Church, ordains only with the consent of the Church, and ordains persons for the service of the Church. Ordination is an ecclesial act from start to finish.

An ordination which is not directed toward pastoral service lacks its ecclesial rooting; it is in a certain sense unreal. Up until the late twelfth century, any ordination which did not lead to pastoral ministry was considered null and void: ordination apart from pastoral ministry was seen as having no sacramental substance. It is only after the twelfth century that the Church came to accept the validity of so-called 'absolute' ordination, that is, of ordinations with no relation to pastoral ministry.[11] The result of this change was precisely the alienation of the clergy from a sense of their integral relation to the whole community of the baptized. They came to be seen more and more as sacramental functionaries who performed specific sacred rites on behalf of the laity. The relation of sacramental authority to pastoral ministry was lost, and a fundamental dislocation in the traditional understanding of ordained ministry was initiated.

The responsibility of the ordained ministries for the celebration of the sacraments is rooted in an essential way in responsible pastoral oversight for a real, human community of faith. Bishops and priests presided over the Eucharist in the early Church because they presided over and were pastorally responsible for, the Christian community. The origin of sacramental responsibility was closely connected to the discernment within the community of the gifts of leadership, and ministerial authority was never detached from the exercise of pastoral responsibility.[12] The sacramental ministrations of the ordained clergy are thus ecclesial acts both in their source and in their end, the building up of the body of Christ. It is in this perspective that the sacramental rites may be seen as the means by which the life of the Christian community is structured.

Concerning Concelebration

As we noted earlier, liturgical customs are sometimes adopted without adequate reflection upon their history or their implications for the potential of the liturgy to mirror an image of the Church. A good example of such a custom is concelebration. In one sense, every celebration of the Eucharist may be called a concelebration, because it involves all members of the community—both laity and clergy—in a single act of thanksgiving to God. All members of the community, without reference to ordained status, are united in the celebration of the Eucharist by virtue of their unity through baptism. It is the Church which celebrates the sacraments. Within that unity there is a mutuality and complementarity of ministries of which the presidential ministry is linked to the work of pastoral oversight in the community. Yet there is a mutuality between lay and ordained ministries; the clergy celebrate in union with the laity—as concelebrants—and not in the place of the laity.

This is not the sense, however, in which the word "concelebration" is used in most instances. In the contemporary Roman Catholic Church, concelebration usually has been understood to refer to an act of co-consecration of the eucharistic elements by a group of ordained priests, and this meaning indicates the reason the practice of sacramental concelebration was authorized for Roman Catholic clergy as part of the large body of liturgical legislation that came out of Vatican Council II. From the middle of the nineteenth century there had been increasingly confirmed in practice the idea that every ordained priest should celebrate the Mass daily, apart from any question of pastoral responsibility of need. Actually this practice had originated in the Middle Ages, especially common from the eighth century, as an act of personal piety on the part of monks. In this context, there was normally no other community for which the individual monks had pastoral responsibility, so these Masses were usually celebrated privately or only with a server.

The custom was not picked up quickly by diocesan clergy, whose piety was only intermittently influenced by such monastic practices, but, in time, the daily Mass became a standard aspect of priestly piety. One encouragement to the extension among parish priests was the elaboration of the stipend system as a basis for clergy support. Whether as a question of piety or of economics, the end result was a highly clericalized and privatized eucharistic piety fostered among the ordained.

In the twentieth century, however, priests living in religious houses and unattached to regular pastoral ministry began to raise questions about the private Mass, which for many came to be seen as a deeply deprived liturgical act, cut off from any clear grounding in corporate prayer. Sacramental concelebration was proposed to deal with this situation and to permit priests both to offer the Mass (and earn the stipend) and at the same time to share it as a corporate act. This was for many priests merely a transitional phase to what was perceived as a better ecclesial form, in which one priest—even in a community of priests— would preside at the daily Eucharist of the community. In practice, it had soon become clear that concelebration as first proposed was experienced far more as a clerical than as an eccesial act. In those situations in which a gathering of laity were also present, this was especially noticeable when a knot of priests gathered around the altar seemed to distance the laity even more than in the past from the liturgical action.

Within Anglicanism, concelebration is yet another example of the takeover of liturgical practice from the Roman rite without adequate consideration of its relevance to Anglican liturgical practice. For the overwhelming majority of Anglican bishops and priests, the idea of an obligatory daily Mass as an act of priestly piety was quite foreign. Fortunately, the celebration of the Eucharist in Anglicanism has always been linked, consciously or unconsciously, to the sacramental needs of a congregation, even when a clericalized model of celebration was in operation. The Anglican context for this question is quite different from that which shaped the Roman Catholic situation. If Rome has been anxious to emphasize the unity of the ordained priesthood, the Anglican situation has permitted a more immediate access to the fully ecclesial concept of the eucharistic celebration. Many Roman Catholic priests today recognize the clerical character of the concelebration legislation so that increasingly, even in situations where many priests are participating in the liturgy, a single priest will preside in the name of the entire community, both laity and clergy, with the awareness that it is the whole people of God who celebrate—it is the Church that celebrates the Eucharist.[13]

Sacraments: Human and Ecclesial

It is impossible in one brief essay to discuss the incredibly wide range of factors that contribute to the shaping of sacramental theology and practice. There are, and this essay has concerned itself with, two dimensions which are fundamental and which, in the end, encompass all of the derivative questions one might want to raise. Those two dimensions are the human and the ecclesial priorities in the shaping of sacramental norms, both in regard to theology and liturgical practice.

The ecclesial priority may be summed up in the idea that it is the whole Church which is the agent of sacramental acts. Sacraments are not the private domain of the clergy but are, rather, a dimension of ministerial responsibility committed to the clergy through ordination. In this view, the sacraments offer a particularly powerful insight into the mutuality of sacramental acts, for in them we see a complementarity of roles which arises from the diversity of gifts (and thus diversity of ministries) which characterizes the body of Christ. The sacraments are ecclesial acts not by virtue of a kind of leveling of ministry so that all participants are involved in precisely the same way, but because of the marvelous diversity of the body which is *imaged* in the complementarity of liturgical roles. The presiding authority of the ordained bishop or priest is an expression of the general oversight and service given and accepted through ordination on behalf of the Church. The clergy are thus, in the classical phrase, "stewards of the mysteries," those within the body called to an explicit responsibility for word and sacrament for the building up of the common life of the body.

This ecclesial dimension of the sacraments is complemented by an equally fundamental dimension in the human aspect of sacramental acts. Ironically, because of the bypath into which sacramental piety has strayed for so long, this human dimension is often given inadequate attention. For those traditions in which sacraments have played an important role, there has been a tendency so to emphasize their sacredness as God's gifts to us that their relation to the principle of incarnation has been slighted. It has almost seemed that to give due regard to their holiness as instruments of grace has required a negligence of their very human forms. But it is precisely this underlying humanness in the sacramental acts, the use of water, oil, bread and wine, the human touch, which reveals the sacraments as extensions of the Incarnation. We do not make the sacraments more sacred by dehumanizing them, by deemphasizing their obvious relation to and grounding in actions basic to our human nature, actions as basic as bathing and eating and drinking. We do no service to a truly incarnational sacramental theology by giving inadequate attention to the role of the flesh in God's work of salvation.[14]

Two sacraments which are probably very seldom connected in theological reflection offer special insight into this human dimension of the sacraments, namely, matrimony and the annointing of the sick. Both of these sacraments have to do in the most obvious ways with our physical humanity, and yet both have been seen by the Church as occasions of critical significance in which the grace of God is instrumentally communicated to us at times which carry what we might call a *natural* significance. The sacraments of matrimony and the anointing of the sick cannot be conceived apart from the reality of the human body. They defy a false spiritualization. They remind us that God touches our lives in every aspect: in the fulfillment of the affective and sexual needs of our nature, and in the crisis of physical illness and the inevitability of physical decay—in love and the generating of new life, and in the giving over of that life in illness and death to the Creator who is the source of our physical existence. By implication, all that is human has the capacity for sanctification. The whole created order, the material world, has the potential of sacrament as an outward, physical sign of the inward and transforming grace of God. Nothing is excluded, neither joy nor pain; all of human life can bear the sign of the divine presence.

This human aspect of the sacraments has been obscured through a kind of sacramental minimalism which has characterized liturgical practice for a number of centuries. A preoccupation with definitions of form and matter and the impact of a need to define minimum standards for sacramental rites celebrated in deprived circumstances has led to the establishment of these minimal standards as "normative" even in otherwise normal situations. This development is especially noticeable with regard to the rites of Initiation. What had once been a long, often three-year, process of incorporation into the body of Christ, became, under the pressure of changed or deprived circumstances, the pouring of water in the Name of the Holy Trinity over the head of a child shortly after its birth if it was in danger of death.

It is easy to understand the concern of parents and of the Church as a whole that a child, especially at a time of high infant mortality in the Middle Ages, should receive the sign of God's favor. But that this minimalist pattern should be generalized under normal circumstances cannot be defended. It has led to privatization of the understanding of God's gift of saving grace. We see in this how a degenerated liturgical practice, in this case the separation of the baptismal sign from the wider framework of the Church's ministry of Christian formation, can turn back upon and reshape the basic theological understanding which the rite is supposed to signify.

Concerning the Eucharist

Sacramental minimalism has also affected the celebration of the Eucharist. It is evident that the human act which under-lies the eucharistic rite is the shared meal. Yet, as we noted earlier, there developed in the Church from about the ninth century the attitude that an emphasis upon the natural parallels to the sacramental acts served to diminish their sacredness. This was a period during which there emerged an insistence upon the *otherness* of sacred realities, and, not surprisingly, it was at this time that the clergy came to be consiously "set apart" from the secular society into a distinct world of clerical privilege.

The liturgical consequences of this attitude were perhaps inevitable given the significance of such ideas for the under-standing of the nature of the Church. Liturgical rites came to be as unlike their natural counterparts as could be imagined. The Eucharist gradually became a sacred meal at which almost no one but the celebrant ate and drank. The alter as a free-standing table became a kind of sacramental shrine of devotion placed against the wall. Perhaps most important of all, since it is a question of the physical matter of the eucharistic species, the bread of the sacrament came to be a self-consciously different bread from the normal bread of the human meal.

The question of the use of leavened bread in the Eucharist strikes some people as a liturgical fad, and it is understandable that at a time of extensive liturgical change much of what has been implemented at the pastoral level has not proved to be of any abiding significance. When it comes to the bread of the Eucharist, however, the issue is one of profound theological and pastoral importance, an importance which cannot be casually dismissed as a fad.

Ordinary, leavened bread continued in use for the Eucharist in Western Christianity until the ninth century, and continues to be used among the Eastern Orthodox today. In the West, the initial reason for change was disciplinary, to assure that clergy would use freshly prepared bread rather than part of a leftover loaf. The solution to the carelessness of clergy was finally the authorization by various meetings of bishops in synod that unleavened bread, that is, a different type of bread from that of the table should be used. Once established in use, unleavened bread came to be identified with the type of bread used by Jesus at the Last Supper, as a kind of repetition of the presumed biblical model. The end of this process, however, was the introduction and use of a different type of bread in the Eucharist. Questions of purity in its preparation became paramount and the bread itself became the bread of angels rather than the spiritual food of men and women. It is not surprising that during this period there developed a serious corrosion of the practice of eucharistic communion among the laity, who were aware of their unworthiness to eat the divinized bread, and that the consecrated host emerged increasingly in a dislocated eucharistic piety as a sacred object to be adored. The eucharistic celebration no longer structured the corporate life of the community of faith in the action of a common meal, and the eucharistic gifts became for most of the laity radically disconnected from the physical intention of their nature as food and drink: "Take, eat; this is my body. Take, drink; this is my blood."

Within Anglicanism, there was a rubrical authorization for the use of leavened bread at the time of the Reformation, but under the influence of the Oxford Movement in the nineteenth century and the subsequent espousal of Roman Catholic liturgical practices, there was a reversion to the use of unleavened bread which was eventually generalized throughout Anglicanism, whether evangelical or catholic in its orientation. Along with its encouragement of the following of Roman Catholic liturgical norms, the High Church revival, very much shaped by the romanticized medievalism which characterized many aspects of nineteenth-century culture, also committed itself to the whole complex of medieval theology and piety of which the liturgical practices were the sign. In other words, Anglican High Churchmen tended to look to Rome for catholic liturgical models and thus took up a highly clericalized pattern. The use of unleavened bread is a potent symbol of the ninth-century mentality in which natural elements are not seen as the normal context of the divine action; rather, physical realities must first be set apart and made different before they are appropriate for use as instruments of grace. It should be obvious that such a mentality suggests a real avoidance of the implications of the Incarnation. A sacramental view in which ordinary things— ordinary bread, ordinary people—can be instruments of grace faces us with God's immediacy to our lives. It is perhaps more reality than we feel we can bear, so we have escaped into sacramental obscurantism. We erect a protective wall between ourselves and the Holy by keeping liturgy remote from the realities of our daily lives.

The human and ecclesial aspects of sacramental practice come together in a particular way in regard to the question of children and the Eucharist. The human aspect of the issue is that the infant is from birth fully a member of his/her family. One only has to observe a parent holding a newborn child to realize the wonderful mystery of our human interdependence. We share a common life; our lives are part of one fabric; our lives coinhere. The infant requires the loving care and nurture of its parents and others if it is to grow into a mature and responsible adult. Yet throughout that whole process the child also affects the lives of the adults through the unique qualities of its own being. There is a mutuality of growth in the common human experience.

This human dimension offers us a fundamental insight into the ecclesial reality. Our rite of baptism clearly states that the baptism of an infant rests upon the committed faith of the adults who present the child to the Church for incorporation into the common life. The infant is not capable, and will not be capable for many years, of making a mature profession of faith. The energy which underlies the pracice of infant baptism is of an incorporation into the family of faith in which the child will be nurtured to maturity, just as we have seen in the basic human pattern of adult responsibility for the newly born. But just as human care includes nourishment of the infant's body, although the child certainly cannot understand the principles of nutrition, so does baptism imply the full incorporation of the child into the life of the family of faith. Baptism is initiation into the communion fellowhip. Not to give the eucharistic gifts to a baptized child is a far greater anomaly than to refrain from infant baptism as well and to await an age at which the child has become adequately mature to make a personal response. It is the rupture between baptism and Eucharist in the case of infants which is the real anomaly.

The familiar response to this idea is that infants do not *understand* the Eucharist well enough to be prepared to receive it. Such an approach does not recognize that it is always God's initiative toward us which first generates a sacramental act. Whether as child or adult, our response is a total human response, the whole being offered to the Creator. Such a response—our oblation of self-giving—is the real substance of our participation in the eucharistic action. It is not uniquely nor even primarily an intellectual response. As the powers of reason develop, they obviously become part of the response of a whole person, but to elevate understanding as a criterion for eucharistic reception is to propose a false intellectualization of the sacramental act. Communion is an act of solidarity within the family of faith. Children are not merely pre-adults; they are fully children, and at every stage of their growth from earliest infancy they manifest their dependence upon the nurturing care of their families, while making their own unique contribution to those around them. There seems to be no reason to exclude such human reciprocity from our understanding of the relationships within the Church.

Children often manifest an unselfconscious openness to the eucharistic gifts from which adults might learn a great deal. Children remind us that liturgy is more than words printed in a book and that sacraments are more than a ritual routine. Communion with the very young is not only important for them as an experience of their spiritual identity with the whole community of faith, it is also important to adults as a perpetual reminder that Jesus has challenged his disciples to "become as little children," and to rest in a loving dependence upon the God who feeds our deepest hunger.

Sacraments of Christ: Christ the Sacrament

The sacraments depend upon the authority of Christ. Their

power and efficacy are derived from his self-offering in death and its transformation in the victory of the resurrection. Death and life—Christ's death and life—are the meanings the sacraments express. Baptism immerses us in his death/life, his paschal mystery, and the Eucharist is the perpetual renewal of that paschal sign by which we are "marked as Christ's own for ever." Our participation in the mystery of Christ is a corporate act because baptism identifies each one of us with the whole people of God. In this sense, the sacraments are instruments of unity because they effect what they signify.

It is because of the organic relation between Christ and the Church that baptism and the Eucharist have been believed to be "instituted of Christ," although in the history of sacramental theology there has existed a rather simplistic notion that Christ explicity instituted baptism and the Eucharist. Until recent years, among Roman Catholic theologians an explicit dominical institution was linked to the other five traditional sacramental acts as well. Sacramental theologians now tend generally to consider the question of the number of the sacraments as a secondary issue, which must be placed within an historical perspective. A more fundamental consideration for contemporary theology is the sacramental nature of the Church as the primary sign of Christ in human history, with any and all sacramental acts (whatever number these may be) seen as explicitations of that underlying sacramental nature. In this perspective it is evident that Jesus implicitly instituted all sacramental acts through the calling forth of a band of disciples who would become the nucleus of a society spread throughout the world yet bound together through their common faith and their incorporation into Christ through the baptismal waters.

Through the sacramental acts of baptism and the Eucharist, and all actions which are the signs of Christ's ministry among us, the unity of the body is structured, shaped as an instrument of transformation and of service in the world. In the end, the foundation for our speaking of sacraments at all is Christ himself, the sacrament of God, the sign of the Father's creative and nurturing presence in the world.

6

Toward an Anglican View of Authority[1]

Arthur A. Vogel

Individuals who call themselves Christians want to live with the authority of Christ in their lives; perhaps better said, they want to live the authority of Christ. Such living is an acknowledgment of dependence on Christ: it is the experience in faith of an authenticating certitude which enables them to face the trials and uncertainty of life with hope and confidence.

If what has been said in the preceding pages about the relation of individual Christians to the community to which they belong is true, that is, if Christians can be themselves only within a community of faith which precedes them and extends beyond them, authority must be found, in a primary sense, in Christian community also. The source of the community's authority is the Spirit of Christ which dwells within it, filling it and leading it into all truth, just as the presence of the Spirit in an individual is the source of that individual's Christian authority.

What we have said serves well enough as definition, but when authority is actually exercised or needs to be identified in interpersonal or intracommunal relationships, problems often arise. Such problems also arise in intercommunal relationships between Churches.

At the communal level, the exercise of authority involves group identity. If a community is to maintain its identity in a world filled with many and various groups and communities, most existing for different purposes, it must have a means of exercising sufficient authority to identify and separate its members from the members of other groups. If a society of bird watchers cannot identify its members and keep them watching birds, it becomes indistinguishable from a soccer club, a transportation union, or a league of bowlers. The authority we are presently describing is a necessary property of any group, secular or religious, but it is of special interest to us in its religious dimension.

Crises of authority are presently found everywhere. We recognize such crises within our personal lives, as we search for a manner of living in troubled times; members of Churches are aware of crises of authority existent within almost every major denomination; and we are aware of the crises of authority existing between the separated Christian Churches. As the ecumenical movement proceeds in its quest of reestablishing the visible unity of God's one, holy, catholic, and apostolic Church, consensus on creedal statements and abstract theological principles is frequently found to be astonishingly easy to achieve. When the Churches begin to consider actually living with each other as one Church, rather than living next to each other as neighbors, however, problems of authority seem quickly to become the chief stumbling blocks.

In its exercise, authority defines a style of living. We all have our own style, and, because it is ours, we do not want someone else to take it away from us or to give us theirs. A most fruitful ecumenical activity, in fact, seems to be that of broadening and deeping our understanding of other peoples' styles rather than changing those styles. As the totality of God's difference from us penetrates the self-consciousness of differing ecclesial communities, those communities are sometimes able to discover enriching differences among themselves where they previously had found only fragmenting division.

Still, basic differences do exist between Churches and not all differences can be euphemized as "enriching."

As Anglicans have participated in the quest for the visible

reunion of the Church, their experience and exercise of authority has confronted and sometimes dumbfounded, if not disappointed, representatives of other Churches with whom they have been in official conversations. Biblicism, as the preceding pages should have illustrated, has never been a characteristic of Anglicanism; on the other hand, although the Churches of the Anglican Communion have maintained the threefold order of bishops, priests, and deacons, and although Anglicans recognize a special teaching office of the episcopate and the other orders of ordained ministry, they have never sanctioned, in their distinctive life, such a teaching office as is attributed to bishops alone in the Roman Catholic Church. Anglicans feel much more at one with the Orthodox Churches in that respect, yet Anglicans have tolerated more differences in their midst than have the Orthodox.

Considering the teaching of theology within the Church, it is not irrelevant to point out that the Anglican Communion has not, on the whole, produced such thick theological tomes or such lengthy theological explications as some of the Western Churches have produced. Theological methodology and a basic way of approaching and understanding God may have more to do with that fact than the inability of Anglican theologians to go on and on. Anglicans have not chosen a single key—be it "faith," "Scripture," "paradox," or a philosophic vocabulary—by which to unlock the manifold problems found in the relationship of human beings to God; they have a tendency to stay closer to biblical language and imagery, in their totality, and to trust less to propositional statement than have some other theological communities.

Acknowledging the situation just described, the following remarks are offered as a context for understanding the Anglican view and exercise of authority.

Any Christian account of authority rightly begins with the statement of the resurrected Jesus recorded in Matthew 28:18, "All authority in heaven and on earth has been given to me."

Christians recognize the authority of Christ to be absolute; no less is implied when they proclaim him to be Lord and Son of God. But it is noteworthy that in all the gospel tradition Jesus did not impose his authority on others in an absolute manner. In fact, he explicitly condemned the rulers of the Gentiles who exercise authority by lording it over their people, imposing authority from above (Mt 20:25; Mk 10:42). Those condemned equated authority with personal power. Christ, on the other hand, did not dictate; instead he taught and persuaded (cf. Mark 1:21f).

As teacher, Jesus was mediator, and authority is essentially mediation. Mediation requires three elements: 1) the thing mediated (truth); 2) the person mediating; and 3) and person or persons receiving the mediation.

If, among the elements we have mentioned, the person mediating is emphasized at the expense of the truth to be mediated, authority is identified with the personal power of the mediator, and so falls under the condemnation of Christ. If, on the other hand, the mediator functions because of his knowledge of the reality to be mediated—that is, its being or truth—then he is an authority because he speaks from that reality, mediating it in a manner consistent with the truth to be known. (The Greek word for authority is *exousia*: it indicates that authority rises "from" or "out of," *ex*, the essence or being, *ousia*, of the thing to be known.)

That Jesus did not impose his authority on people in a absolute manner is evident throughout the gospel tradition. As a first instance we may notice the characteristic way he taught by parable. Parables are simple stories of particular events from which the storyteller is completely removed; the subject matter itself speaks to the hearers in a decisive way, lighting their lives in circumstances they recognize to be similar to theirs. The concreteness of the stories used in parables is important; parables are not reducible to abstract truths or principles from which the details of life have been removed. Parables speak to us where we are in the totality of our lives.

The use of miracles by Christ in the apostolic tradition is also significant. Although Christ's miracles cause wonderment, the tradition never reduces them to wonders. The miracles are primarily signs indicating something beyond themselves; they are sometimes called "powers," but they are not displays of power for its own sake. They signify, and so teach, the power of God— who is love.

At the moment of his betrayal by Judas, Jesus was seen by the earliest Christian community refusing to assert his authority by power alone; thus we read that he refused to call the legions of angels from the Father for his defense (Mt 26:53).

Most significantly of all, and qualifying everything that has just been said, is the sense in which the resurrection was the beginning of the whole gospel tradition. All of the Gospels, and indeed the entire New Testament, were written in witness to Jesus as Lord after—and because of—his resurrection. Here is found the primary Christian instance where being or reality itself furnishes the authority for words spoken about it—even the words of Jesus. Had Jesus not risen from the dead his words would have carried no more authority than those of any other human being. But he did rise from the dead, and the reality of that truth enlightened and authorized all that he had said before his death; so it is that the gospel tradition is post-Easter in its origin and intention even when it describes pre-Easter events.

Even the authority of the teachings of Jesus had to await their justification from a reality which existed beyond them. But once the authority of Jesus as teacher was shown by the resurrection, truth was seen to have been mediated so uniquely through him that the mediator became accepted as the thing mediated: it was said that "God became man," and the event was called the Incarnation.

Since all authority has been given to Christ, Christian authority is found in individuals when the Spirit of Christ is found in them. Christians become mediators of Christ in the quality and holiness of their lives when his reality shines through them. His truth justifies and authorizes them; thus authority in its root meaning (*exousia*) is present.

As convincing and compelling as the holiness of an individual may be, however, a person is able to live the authority of Christ only as he or she belongs to a community of faith. As has been indicated, Christians believe individuals are saved by becoming members of God's own people, a chosen race, a holy nation; Christians know the Church as the New Israel called into existence by a New Covenant between God and human beings (cf. I Peter 2:9). The Father who sent his only begotten Son into the world is a God who has entered history in one specific way and in one specific place, and it is only by accepting the uniqueness of God's revelation in Christ that one is able to be a Christian.

All of this means that no one can be a Christian by himself or herself alone; individual identity in Christ depends on a communal memory, a vocabulary, and a discernment which precedes the believer, locating him or her in relationship with God and making him or her dependent on the experience and witness of other people. As has also been indicated, the Bible became a canon of books by communal acceptance, and only within that acceptance is the Bible the normative record of the apostolic witness to Jesus as the Christ.

An individual's life of faith cannot help but depend upon a community of faith. Faith itself, we have said, is openness to God—a simple definition to be sure, but one inclusive enough to convey the fullness of its meaning even in the thought of Paul. "Faith" so defined is obviously a life to be lived, not a proposition to be repeated.

When faith is considered in this basic manner, the problem which confronts us is how to maintain the openness it requires at both the individual and communal levels. The need for openness to God in our individual lives is obvious enough; the quest for such openness is one way of describing our on-going spiritual pilgrimage. But there must also be a lived openness to God on the part of a community if that community is truly to be a community *of faith*. Such openness is perhaps most obviously seen as a community gathers to worship a God beyond it, but the whole life of a community of faith must in some manner exhibit an openness to its transcendent and mysterious Source.

A primary difficulty in maintaining the openness of which we are speaking is the fact that both individuals and communities express themselves in propositions; as the identity of common experience is preserved through the passing of time, the temptation constantly arises to reduce lived openness to formal propositions. Propositions do not change and consequently are a great help in establishing identity through time; such identity is crucially important when adherence to a past revelation accepted as an unchanging norm is in question.

A tension thus arises between what has been called "faith"

and what has been called "religion." "Faith" is a lived openness to the mysterious and transcendent Source of all, while "religion" refers to the necessary elaboration in human terms of an originating revelation. Jacques Ellul has offered many penetrating insights into the tension we are describing, and he has found many of the same elements in the tension that he discovered in his famous analysis of technological society. For example, even though a revelation in itself may be utterly personal, its human elaboration will always contain impersonal, even mechanical, elements. Conceptually elaborated structures of belief and codes of ethics tend to become institutionalized and self-perpetuating precisely as political power does; of itself, all such institutionalized power tends to multiply, centralize, and universalize. Such power tends to exercise absolute authority in the name of complete certainty, demanding unquestioning servitude and requiring condemnation of those who differ from it.

Such an analysis of the absolutizing and self-perpetuating nature of institutions does not deny that formal expression and institutional organization are necessary in the formation of human communities; rather, it highlights a dynamic which constantly occurs within the Church when it is considered on the one hand as a self-transcending community open to God's mysterious presence and on the other hand as an organization whose institutions are the repository of past experience. The Church always has both self-perpetuating and self-transcending dimensions within it. The question at issue is how to keep the authority of the Ultimate as the authority of faith instead of letting the authority of a human organization become ultimate. Put in different words, we need to insure that the authority of faith is the authority of the Ultimate and not the authority of a worldly organization.

It is important to stress again—and constantly to keep in mind—that all Churches seek the mean beween these extremes. The danger is twofold. The presence of transcendent Mystery alone immobilizes individuals and communities, allowing them to say nothing in human terms. Such moments are necessary for our religious lives, supplying nothing less than the origin and context for religion, but speech and direction must issue from such mystical silence or God's purpose in placing us in the world is contradicted. The other danger consists in acknowledging the mysterious origin and context of religion, and then going on to reduce the acknowledged Mystery to formal, abstract statements.

By intention, we all desire the mean between the extremes. An individual or Church which says anything has to some extent avoided the first danger we have described; the most likely danger to occur in the lives of individuals and Churches in the second. Who of us has not been guilty of saying too much? Words are easier to produce than deeds. Since Churches are organizations, the tendency towards organizational self-perpetuation through institutions (the latter sometimes being a synonym for bureaucracy) is obvious. To take as examples the Anglican Communion and Roman Catholic Church, it might be observed that the besetting sin of Anglican Churches as Churches is to say too little—and frequently for the wrong reason—and the besetting sin of individual Anglicans is to say too much—frequently for the right reasons! On the other hand, many feel that the Roman Catholic Church says too much as a Church and that frequently , within it, individuals say—or are allowed to say—too little.

An apparently radical difference in the exercise of authority is found between the Anglican Church and the Roman Catholic Church, owing to the manner in which the Roman Catholic Church has proclaimed its power to teach infallibly. The "infallibility of the Pope" is both a rallying point and battle cry for Christians, and the nature of authority in the Church can be clarified by examining the issues it involves.

Instead of looking at a specific theological or conciliar definition, I should like to set up a model to illustrate the type of argument I find most frequently employed in explications of infallibility. For purposes of discussion, I will attempt to establish a typology I believe to be typical.

A common explication of the infallibility of the Church begins, as it no doubt should, with the abiding presence of the Spirit in the Church. Because the Spirit abides in the Church, it is argued, the Church is led to the unerring (infallible) proclamation and (re)formulation of the gospel, the revelation given to the saints.

There is a sense in which that statement must be true, and in that sense every Christian should accept it. If the statement is false, there can be no individual salvation in Christ, for we only know Christ within and by means of the community of faith. If there is no unity between Christ and his Church, we cannot know Christ.

The claim of the Church's unerring ability to proclaim and formulate the gospel does not go as far as many people mistakenly believe. The claim does not, for example, mean that the Church can in any way add to the truth of revelation; in reformulating the gospel the Church must only clarify what has already been given to it. That is why the apostolic witness recorded in Scripture is normative for all subsequent proclamation and clarification. Clarifications of revelation made by the Church may have "lasting value," as ecumenical discussion has put it,[2] but because human words can never capture or exhaust the divine Word, certain types of human reformulation of the faith are theoretically without limit. The unerring, lasting value of conciliar clarifications of the faith comes from excluding human accretions to—and intrusions into—the gospel, rather than finally formulating the gospel (as has also been indicated in ecumenical discussion).[3]

But there is still more to be said. Upon closer analysis, the opening statement about the Spirit's presence in the Church is less a point of departure than a subject for inquiry. We should ask what it means for the Spirit to "abide" in the Church. In what manner is the Spirit present? Then, instead of arguing that "because" the Spirit abides in the Church certain consequences follow, it would be more accurate to say that "insofar as" the Spirit abides in the Church certain consequences result. Finally, we need to inquire into the nature of the revelation or faith or deposit that is said to be given once and for all to the Church.

Do not Christians believe that the ultimate revelation of God to human beings is a person, Jesus the Christ? The person is called God's Word, but the fullness of the Word is the person— not the propositions he utters, not the propositions spoken about him. The fact that the Spirit abides in the Church is significant because it is the Spirit of Christ sent from the Father, a mark of Christ's own divinity, who is given to the Church. As we have seen, all authority has been given to Jesus, and since Jesus gives his Spirit to the Church, how the Spirit abides in the Church is dependent on how Jesus is the Son of God. How God is in the Church is dependent upon how God is in Christ; thus, as should be the case in a religion which believes in an incarnate Lord, questions of ecclesiology are ultimately dependent upon questions of Christology.

All authority is Christ's to be sure; but how do we know Christ? To say that "God became man" or that the Word became flesh means that somehow God entered our world and became wholly contextual with us. In Christ our human reality totally opens to the "more" of God. But how can that be expressed?

The two possible answers to that question are "by propositions" and "by symbols." Propositions are formal; they are analytic and abstract in nature, aiming at conceptual clarity. A symbol, on the other hand, is more evocative than formally analytic; it is concrete rather than abstract; and it relies on images rather than concepts.

The propositional and symbolic modes of discourse illustrate two types of Christology found in the life of the church. The attempt to describe how God was in Christ can be made by using either propositions or symbols. (The fact is that a combination of the two is necessary, but for long periods of time symbols were not regarded as a unique manner of signification and were thought to be reducible without remainder to propositional statements. Think of the scholastic manuals of theology found for centuries in the Western Church.)

A propositional understanding of Christ, we suggest, leads to a propositional understanding of authority in the Church. However, with the new and renewed appreciation of the uniqueness of religious symbols—recognizing that they convey true but nonpropositional dimensions of reality—certain formalistic expectations inherited from previous epochs should be recognized for their inadequacy, as should the type of authority they foster.

The great images of faith, the inexhaustible symbols of Christ's nature and role among us which nourish, support, and lead us—*resurrection, Lord, Son of God, Son of Man, Savior, Redeemer, ascension,* to name but a few—have a symbolic richness and comprehension that cannot be reduced to abstract, formal statements. The great images of faith are concrete, moving images in time, as Jesus himself and our lives are in time. They are not static structures, which can be more clearly delineated in abstract terms; the great images of faith are more perfect and revealing than are ideas abstracted from them. The use of parables by Christ has a direct affinity with the symbolic Christology we are describing, while the essentialism of certain theological manuals offers a splendid example of propositional Christology.

Symbolic images have the wholeness and mystery of persons about them, and so, precisely because of their *ambiguities*, they are more adequate vehicles for the mystery of God's revelation than formal propositions are. The manner in which such images transcend propositions is analogous to the way God transcends our world; thus symbols help keep us open to the transcendent Other.

The manner in which we can best apprehend Jesus as the Son of God is a criterion for the type of certitude and clarity we can expect of the Church—his mystical body in the world. Jesus and our understanding of him are the source of everything Christian, and conclusions originating in him as their premise cannot contain more clarity than their source.

Even though we cannot clearly understand how Jesus is Son of God, we believe it is conceptually possible to indicate the importance of the finite, human world in the light of the use God has made of it in the revelation of his Son. Statements about faith and morals can and must be made because of the use of the finite by the infinite, but the finite must never become ultimate in the statements. A revelation is a revelation precisely because in it the finite is shown to be contingent and totally dependent on something beyond itself; that is an existential truth and its acknowledgement should be more than merely formal. Human dependency on God must be operative in everything Christian; it must, for example, determine the way a revelation is given, presented, passed on, and evaluated. Only under these conditions can *God's* authority be discovered in human lives and in the Church.

An illustration of our typology can be found in the Dogmatic Constitution on the Church of Vatican II:

> The body of the faithful as a whole, annointed as they are by the Holy One (cf. 1 John 2:20,27), cannot err in matters of

belief. Thanks to a supernatural sense of the faith which characterizes the People as a whole, it manifests this unerring quality when "from the bishops down to the last member of the laity" it shows universal agreement in matters of faith and morals.[4]

It is from such a statement about the infallibility of the Church as a whole that Roman Catholic theology proceeds to justify and explicate the infallibility of the Pope. Accordingly, before proceeding to the papal doctrine, we should highlight the principal contentions of the quotation above.

Reference to the universal nature of the Church should be especially noted: it is the *faithful as a whole* who cannot err; the "supernatural sense of the faith" that prevents error belongs to the *People as a whole*; and, as is further stated, the unerring ability of the Church is manifest when there is *universal agreement* "in matters of faith and morals." Infallibility is willed for the Church, then, only in its entirety and only in the area of faith and morals. Infallibility, as should be well known by now, is operative only in restricted circumstances about a restricted subject matter.

Turning to the infallibility of the Pope, many helpful clarifications have been made in recent years by Roman Catholic theologians. Some of the clarifications have resulted from the work of Vatican II and some have come from a more adequate understanding of Vatican I. Whatever function and role the Pope has in the Roman Catholic Church is now accorded to him because he is the Bishop of Rome; he is thus placed firmly within the Church and within the college of his fellow bishops. It is then maintained that the Bishop of Rome, only as head of and in union with the college of bishops, voices that infallibility which belongs to the Church as a whole. Inability to err is not a personal power he possesses.

As we have indicated, such explications are helpful and encouraging. As far as definition goes, things are in good order. The difficulty that remains for some lies not in the realm of words, but in process. Infallibility describes a function; it has to do with the way people act in making judgments. It occurs at the level of full human experience, not at the level of propositions and definitions—in the realm of "faith," not the realm of "religion." We are back at the tension which exists between lived openness to the transcendent mystery of God and the self-perpetuating nature of the Church as an institution.

How are we to resolve this tension?

The first thing to be said is that such a resolution is impossible if it is thought that the tension can be made to disappear; the tension is a part of the human condition. The tension, in other words, is a part of the reality of our world, and in our world we believe there is but one way to make progress in the face of it. The first thing we must recognize, as most theologians do, is that the infallibility of the Church basically and empirically depends upon the indefectibility of the Church, that is, on the Church's lasting nature and inability to fail. It is the presence of the Spirit in the Church which makes the Church indefectible. But I believe we must go further.

The claim that the Church is infallible is not true by definition; nor is it a purely formal statement with the nature of a mathematical definition. To claim that the Church is infallible is to make a claim about an empiral reality in the world. The claim has a content going beyond its words and so must be capable of some kind of empirical verification if it is reasonably to be accepted as true.

I contend that, when considered from the point of view of empirical verification, the life of the Church is precisely the same with regard to both indefectibility and infallibility. Looked at empirically, in other words, infallibility is reducible to indefectibility—with no remainder.

If faith is not to be reduced to either credulity or fantasy, it must be subject to some kind of verification in the course of history, and the only nondefinitional, historical verification for infallibility is indefectibility. Indefectibility, in fact, is the lone empirically operative criterion for the truth of Christianity itself; that is why, as Paul put it, if Christ has not been raised from the dead then we of all people are most to be pitied (I Cor 15:19). Words are not enough.

A theory of infallibility may formally save itself by claiming there is an a priori or implicit consent of the Church already given when a binding pronouncement is made, but only time and experience will tell whether or not the consent is actually present. The claim that it is present may be mistaken. History furnishes us with examples of councils which were called to be general (ecumenical) but which were not so accepted by the Church; and there have also been councils not representative of the whole Church which turned out to be accepted as general. The council held at Constantinople in 381, now known as the Second Ecumenical Council, was convoked as no more than an Eastern general synod; its recognition by the wider Church is what has enabled it to be listed as a General Council. Among councils convoked ahead of time to be general that were not accepted as such by the Church are the Imperial Synod of Sardica (343), Arles (314), and Ephesus II (449).

We have seen the correlation between universal acceptance by the Church and the infallibility of the Church in *Lumen Gentium*. We believe that identification to be a sound one, for in it the expression of oneness required of the community is an analogue of the oneness which belongs to the Truth in which Christians believe. Universality of acceptance is an objective test for the persuasive force of Truth; it is a way the power of Truth can be shown to be more than the claim of one individual. In the realm of faith, universal acceptance plays a role analogous to empirical verification by scientific researchers. Universal acceptance is a way truth is able to speak in its name—here, in God's name—rather than in the name of one human being who claims his view is true; such "objectivity" of truth is precisely what ought to be according to the root meaning of "authority." Authority, remember, ultimately arises from the nature of reality itself, not from the claim of an individual alone: It must be acknowledged that "universal consent" is not always easy to determine. Heretics and dissenters have existed throughout the Church's life, and sooner or later some criterion other than claimed "openness to God" must be employed to determine who is within a visible community and who is outside of it. A community must be one thing rather than another if it is to have any meaningful identity in the world. But such problems are empirical problems and can be decided on an empirical basis. Our concern has been to show that "infallibility," for all of its formal precision, has no verifiable, empirical connotation that can establish its truth. Thus, even with its attendant difficulties, a Church *in via* should not expect more than indefectibility and the type of infallibility which is verifiably reducible to indefectibility.

As the resurrection was to the teaching of Jesus, so universal consent is to the teaching of the Church. We have no personal control over the resurrection of Christ or over the universal consent of the Church; in each instance a reality independent of us speaks to us, and, as a consequence, authority cannot be reduced to human power lording it over others.

Would it be too much to say that the Church should desire nothing more than indefectibility and the assurance of truth it entails, since Christ's rising from the dead is his indefectibility—and we can do no more than live in him? After all, Jesus' resurrection—his indefectibility—not his opinions about the authorship of the psalms or the time of the parousia, is the sole guarantee of our salvation in him.

7

Looking to the Future

Arthur Michael Ramsey

It will have been apparent to the readers of the essays in this book that the characteristic theology of Anglicans is grounded not on a confessional position akin to other confessions of the Reformation, but rather upon a conviction that the Anglican Church claims identity and continuity with the Church of the Scriptures and the fathers, and is called to teach and to live the faith to which the Scriptures and the fathers witness. Thus the Thirty-nine Articles had their significance not as a confessional definition but as an aid to the recovery of the scriptural and primitive faith, a recovery which indeed demanded the saying of Yea or Nay to some of the controversial positions of the time. But Anglican theologians soon found themselves not only saying Yea or Nay but looking behind and beneath some of the controversies of the sixteenth century and the assumptions behind them. This took time, and as Dean Church said in his fascinating essay on Lancelot Andrewes, the English Reformation included the divines of the seventeenth as well as those of the sixteenth century. Not least is it significant that in exploring antiquity Anglicans looked to East as well as to West, and the readiness to look to the East became significant in the later ecumenical scene.

In this work of exploration and exposition, Anglican theologians have been concerned both with the past and with the contemporary in the understanding of tradition in successive cultural settings. We see this twofold concern in Richard Hooker and it has been present in Anglicanism ever since. Inevitably, there came tensions and controversies concerning the relation of Scripture and tradition and the relation of both to new knowledge of the world. But from the time of Hooker till today two special characteristics of the Anglican way have been apparent, and both their distinctive witness and the interplay between them have helped to shape the Anglican story and to determine the Anglican role in Christendom.

The first of these characteristics has been the bond between theology and spirituality. It is very significant that the formularies of the Church of England included not only the Articles but the Ordinal and the *Book of Common Prayer* as well. The Church's theology is thus closely related to the Church's worship, prayer, and spiritual life and with the work of the pastoral priesthood. The inquirer about the Church of England was invited not only to study the documents but to share in the worship. This characteristic of Anglicanism represents the true role of the Christian theologian. He is called, by the very nature of theology, not only to cerebral processes of study and teaching, but to the knowledge of God which comes by prayer and contemplation. While this aspect of the theologian has not always been apparent it has been seen in a long line of Anglican divines, specially perhaps in the seventeenth and nineteenth centuries. If it is sometimes hard to see today, there are still many signs of hope.

The other characteristic has been a reverence for the human reason, not only as part of the process of knowledge but as an aspect of Man created in God's own image. For while some of the Reformed theologians have seemed to separate God and man unduly, Anglicans, without belittling the distinction of creator and creature, have often dwelt upon the Affinity of Man to his Creator, and this has sometimes been linked with a kind of Christian humanism related to the divine Word by whom all things are made. But there are limits; and where and how are they to be found? Here the first Anglican characteristic comes as an aid, helping the *Lex Credendi* by the *Lex Orandi* as the heart of Christianity is the worship of the God who became incarnate.

The interaction of these two trends has often been apparent

in Anglican history. Sometimes in conflict, these trends have served one another. The critical reason can help to free worship from fancy and false sentiment, and the spirit of worship can help the critical mind to find the agnosticism of awe and mystery. Perhaps no Anglican has written more movingly on both these themes than F. J. A. Hort in his Hulsean Lectures (1871) entitled *The Way, the Truth, the Life*. Hort wrote: "Truth of revelation remains inert till it has been appropriated by a human working of recognition which it is hard to distinguish from that of discovery." Again, he said, "The earth as well as the heavens is full of God's glory, so that every addition to truth becomes a fresh opportunity for adoration."

What of the future? Today the Anglican theologian faces the challenge of the ecumenical scene, and the challenge of the Christian role in a stormy and catastrophic world.

In the ecumenical scene the Anglican brings convictions inherent in his own tradition: the appeal to the ancient Church, readiness to learn from East as well as from West, an awareness of our debt to the Reformation, an appreciation of much which the Church of Rome conserves and of the significance of the Second Vatican Council, and at least the linking of theology with spirituality and an openness to the many aspects of contemporary thought. Like others he is aware that some theological issues cut right across the divisions of Christendom, and he is aware, too, of the eschatological aspect of Christianity: "It does not yet appear what we shall be."

Yet the unity to which Christians are called is far more than theologican synthesis and structural oneness. In the seventeenth chapter of St. John, Jesus prays for the unity of the disciples in truth, in holiness, in mission to the world, and in the indwelling of the Son and the Father. The truth of God revealed in the incarnation is one with the indwelling of the incarnate Son in the lives of the disciples, and this is indeed the meaning of the Holy Catholic Church. Hence unity involves the renewal of lives in the worship of God, in the service of humanity, and in the holiness of which heaven is the goal. As Ireneus said, "The glory of God is a living man, the life of man is the vision of God."

Just as the Anglican today is caught in the ecumenical scene, so like all Christians he is caught in the scene of world history. To be an Anglican is to belong to a communion no longer limited by the English language or Anglo-Saxon culture. It is to belong to a family of Christians consisting of many races and cultures, to a world where nations and people are involved in violence, where weapons of destruction exist and continue to be made, and where luxury and hunger abide side by side. It is in this world that the theologian is exploring the meaning of the incarnation of God and the coming of the Kingdom of God in the world. To be a theologian is to be exposed to the vision of heaven and to the tragedies of mankind. But the theologian will not be startled by this for he knows that, in the words of F. C. Burkitt, "Christianity was from the first organized for a time of catastrophe," and that the divine sovereignty in the world is by the way of self-sacrifice. To the pure in heart there is the promise of the vision of God.

Notes

Chapter 2. Reason, Faith, and Mystery

[1]Cf. Austin Farrer, "Revelation," in *Faith and Logic*, ed. Basil Mitchell (London: George Allen & Unwin Ltd., 1957), pp. 89ff.

[2]Cf. Austin Farrer, *Saving Belief* (London: Hoder and Stoughton, 1964), pp. 11 – 34 *passim*.

[3]St. *Thomas Aquinas, Summa Theologica*. I, q. 3, Prologue.

[4]Ibid., I, q. 2, a. 3, Respondeo.

[5]Cf. William G. Pollard, *Chance and Providence* (New York: Charles Scribner's Sons, 1958), *passim*.

[6]Austin Farrer, *The Glass of Vision* (London: Dacre Press, 1958), p. 49.

[7]Ibid., p. 51.

Chapter 3. Jesus Christ: God with Us

[1]"In the care he shows for man and his record of suffering, for publicans and sinners, for the poor, the crippled and the blind, for the oppressed and for people torn apart by 'evil spirits', Jesus is a living parable of God: that is how God cares for man. In the story of Jesus is told the story of God. It is God himself who opens up to us in the story that is the life of Jesus a new world, a different experience of reality and way of living: thus the New Testament story *about* Jesus forms the response of the first Christians to the story *of* Jesus himself." Edward Schillebeeckx, *Jesus: An Experiment in Christology* (New York: Seabury, 1979), p. 159.

[2]For a brief description of the religious scene in the first century, see J. N. D. Kelly, *Early Christian Doctrines*, rev. ed. (San Francisco: Harper and Row, 1978, chap. 1.

[3]Schillebeeckx, p. 438.

[4]In his important and recent books, *The Point of Christology* (San Francisco:

Harper and Row, 1982), Schubert M. Ogden makes a similar point. He criticizes some contemporary Christologies for being exclusively concerned with the history of Jesus, that is, what we can know about him through an investigation of the biblical sources, as important as that may be, but neglecting the significance of Jesus for those who believe in him. Both, he argues, are part of the data with which Christology must deal: "[The question which Christology answers] is not only a question about Jesus but also, and at the same time, a question about the meaning of ultimate reality for us. Thus it is what I call an *existential-historical* question, meaning thereby the kind of question that does indeed ask about what has actually happened, but that does so in such a way as to ask about its meaning for us here and now in the present rather than about its being in itself then and there in the past" (p. 39).

[5] For a discussion of this movement in the New Testament, see James D. G. Dunn, *Christology in the Making* (Philadelphia: Westminster, 1980), chap. 4.

[6] Dunn, p. 255. Dunn denies that Paul's Christology asserts a doctrine of pre-existence. For an answer to Dunn, see Anthony Tyrrell Hanson, *The Image of the Invisible God* (London: SCM, 1982), chap. 3.

[7] Dunn, p. 256.

[8] On the appropriateness of development in Christology, see, C. F. D. Moule, *The Origin of Christology* (Cambridge: Cambridge University Press, 1977).

[9] A thorough study of the controversies leading to the Council of Chalcedon can be found in A. Grillmeier, *Christ in the Christian Tradition*, 2d rev. ed. (Atlanta: John Knox, 1975), vol. 1.

[10] See, for example, his *Orations against the Arians*, Book III, 32 and 33. Cited in Richard A. Norris, Jr., *The Christological Controversy* (Philadelphia: Fortress, 1980), p. 91. Athanasius goes on to develop the image of Christ as the Second Adam and prototype of the new humanity.

[11] For a helpful summary of the contemporary debate, see Hanson, chap. 1.

[12] *De Incarnatione* VII. Cited in Grillmeier, p. 432.

[13] Or. ad Dominas 31. cited in Grillmeier, p. 477.

[14] For a lucid and helpful exegesis of the Definition, see Richard A. Norris, Jr., *Understanding the Faith of the Church* (New York: Seabury, 1979), pp. 167 – 69. The text of the Definition can be found in *The Book of Common Prayer*, p. 864.

[15] See, for example, A. M. Ramsey, *From Gore To Temple: An Era in Anglican Theology* (New York: Scribner, 1960); William J. Wolf, ed., *The Spirit of Anglicanism* (Wilton, Connecticut: Morehouse-Barlow, 1979); and James E. Griffiss, *Church, Ministry and Unity: A Divine Commission* (Oxford: Blackwell, 1983).

[16] The most obvious example in recent theological literature has been the development of Jürgen Moltmann's Christology from *The Crucified God* (New York: Harper & Row, 1974) through *The Trinity and the Kingdom of God* (London: SCM, 1981).

[17]See, for example, A. M. Allchin, *The Kingdom of Love and Knowledge* (London: Darton, Longman, & Todd, 1979) and Ernest C. Miller, Jr., "The Pentecost Sermons of Lancelot Andrewes: An Ecumenical Agenda," *Anglican Theological Review* (July 1983), pp. 306 – 23.

[18]On the use of *persona* to translate *hypostasis*, see Thomas Aquinas, *Summa Theologiae* 1a, 29, 3 and 3a, 2, 2 and 3.

[19]A history of the concept of "person" can be found in Karl Rahner, ed., *Encyclopedia of Theology: The Concise Sacramentum Mundi* (New York: Seabury, 1975). Also, on the continuity between the patristic and contemporary meanings, see Vladimir Lossky, *The Mystical Theology of the Eastern Church* (London: J. Clarke, 1957), p. 53.

[20]See Schillebeeckx, pp. 256 – 71. See also John Bowker, *The Sense of God* (Oxford: Clarendon, 1973).

[21]For an excellent discussion of the last words from the Cross, see Walter Kasper, *Jesus the Christ* (New York: Paulist, 1976), p. 118.

[22]Gregory Nanzianzen, *Ep.* 101, 7. Cited in Kelly, p. 297.

[23]Shillebeeckx, p. 212.

[24]It is interesting to note that the story of the woman caught in adultery, whether or not it formed an original part of the Fourth Gospel, came to be associated with Jesus' discourse to the Pharisees concerning himself as the light of the world whose judgment is true (Jn 8:12ff.). This is also a major theme of the 1 Letter of John.

[25]Karl Rahmer, *Theological Investigations*, (Baltimore: Helicon Press, 1966), vol. 4, p. 128.

[26]Although I cannot deal with the subject here, it is in such a context, I believe, that the several stories of the Transfiguration ought to be understood.

[27]See Dunn, chap. 4.

[28]Thomas F. Torrance, *Space, Time and Resurrection* (Grand Rapids, Michigan: Eerdmans, 1976), p. 129. This is a study of the resurrection which I have found very helpful. H. M. Relton, writing earlier in this century, made a similar point: "The key to the Universality of Christ's manhood lies in its truly human character, and the key to its truly human character lies in the fact that it was truly Divine. It was the humanity of the Son of God himself. If in the Person of Christ the humanity of God is revealed, this can only be that humanity which pre-existed, that human element which is in God. Christ's humanity is a revelation of God's nature . . . The Incarnation, if it is a revelation of Deity in humanity, is nonetheless a revelation of humanity in Deity: only thus can it be also a revelation of man's true relationship to God." *A Study in Christology* (London: SPCK, 1929), p. 251.

Chapter 5. The Structure of Christian Community

[1]*Summa Theologiae*, Q.35, A.3, *Sed contra*. Thomas continues in the *Responsio*: "The character of baptism gives one the power to receive the other sacraments." It is thus baptism which establishes the sacramental structuring of the Christian life.

[2]*On the Resurrection*, 8. Tertullian goes on in this passage to show the intimate relation between the internal and external dimensions of Christian Initiation, and in so doing epitomizes the 'sacramental idea.'

[3]Cf., for example, Theophilus Dorrington (? – 1715), *A Familiar Guide to the Right and Profitable Receiving of the Lord's Supper* (London, 1695), pp. 37 – 38, where we find,

> By Baptism we are admitted into this Covenant, and make our first solemn acceptance of it. By the Lord's Supper we renew it, if it has been broken on our part by any wilful sin committed since we were baptized: or else we therein testify and declare our continuance still in it, and our purpose and desire to do so.

[4]Such a failure of faith may be found even in New Testament times as, for example, when the Epistle to the Hebrews speaks of those who apostatize, 6:4 – 8.

[5]The most useful survey of the entire process of the disintegration of the integrity of the rites of Christian Initiation remains *Christian Initiation. Baptism in the Medieval West* by J. D. C. Fisher (London, 1965).

[6]There has been a constantly growing literature on this subject. Note especially the following: M. J. Hatchett, "The Rite of 'Confirmation' in The Book of Common Prayer and in *Authorized Service 1973*," *ATR* (July 1974), pp. 292 – 310; L. L. Mitchell, "The Theology of Christian Initiation and *The Proposed Book of Common Prayer*," *ATR* (October 1978), pp. 399 – 419. L. L. Mitchell, "What is Confirmation?" *ATR* (April 1973), pp. 201 – 12. M. H. Shepherd, "Confirmation: The Early Church," *Worship* (January 1972), pp. 15 – 20. L. Weil, "Confirmation: Some Notes on Its Meaning," *ATR* (April 1977), pp. 220 – 24.

[7]Cf. Nathan Mitchell, *Cult and Controversy: The Worship of the Eucharist Outside Mass* (New York, 1982), which, through the presentation of material extending beyond the apparent limitation implied by the title, offers a remarkable overview of the evolution of the understanding of the Eucharist from sacramental action of the assembled community to adoration of divinized bread.

[8]Cf. Louis Weil, *Sacraments & Liturgy: The Outward Signs* (Oxford, 1983), pp. 37 – 39.

[9]Cf. Joseph A. Jungmann, S.J., *The Mass of the Roman Rite: Its Origin and Development*, vol. 1 (New York, 1951), p. 465, n. 17. This revered work traces in detail the origin and development of all aspects of the Western eucharistic rite, and through this historical method offers splendid insight into the way liturgical

rites develop under the influence of a range of factors. The study thus gives us a certain perspective to these ritual details for establishing a method of evaluation as to their continued value in the liturgical practice of today.

[10]Cf. Hans von Campenhausen, *Ecclesiastical Authority and Spiritual Power* (London, 1969), surveys the transformation of the concept of authority as exercised by the leaders of the Church in the first three centuries.

[11]Cf. Cyrille Vogel, "An Alienated Liturgy," in *Liturgy: Self-Expression of the Church*, Consilium, vol. 72, ed. H. Schmidt (New York, 1972), pp. 18 – 21. See also, Cyrille Vogel, *Ordinations inconsistantes et caractère inadmissible* (Torino, 1978).

[12]Cf. Hervé-Marie Legrand, "The Presidency of the Eucharist According To the Ancient Tradition," in *Worship*, vol. 53, no. 5 (September 1979), pp. 413 – 38. See also, Edward J. Kilmartin, S.J., "Apostolic office: Sacrament of Christ," in *Theological Studies*, vol. 36, No. 2 (June 1975), pp. 243 – 64.

[13]For an excellent summary of the subject from an Anglican point of view, cf. Trevor Lloyd and Hugh Wybrew: "Concelebration in the Eucharist," General Synod [of the Church of England] pamphlet no. 163 (London, 1982).

[14]Louis Bouyer has explored the medieval situation in which the human signs of the sacraments came to be played down in behalf of an emphasis on their otherness, their difference from the physical dimensions of daily life. Cf. *Rite and Man* (Notre Dame, 1963).

Chapter Chapter 6. Toward an Anglican View of Authority

[1]Adapted from "Christ's Authority And Ours," in *Ecumenical Trends*, vol. 9, no. 10 (November 1980) and *The Anglican Theological Review*, vol. 63, no. 1 (January 1981). Used by permission.

[2]Anglican-Roman Catholic International Commission, *An Agreed Statement on Authority in the Church I*, in *The Final Report* (Cincinnati, Ohio: Forward Movement Publications, 1982).

[3]Ibid., 19.

[4]Second Vatican Council, *Dogmatic Constitution on the Church*, 12, in *The Documents of Vatican II*, Walter M. Abbott, S.J., Gen. Ed. (Guild Press, American Press, Association Press, 1966).

Contributors

HENRY CHADWICK is Regius Professor Emeritus of Divinity, University of Cambridge, and former Dean of Christ Church, Oxford. He holds honorary doctorate degrees from Yale University and the University of Chicago, and is a member of the American Academy of Arts and Sciences. He is also a Fellow of the British Academy and he has been appointed to the first and second International Anglican Roman Catholic Commissions. Dr. Chadwick is an internationally recognized expert in the history of Christian thought, and has special interest in the New Testament and patristic periods. Among his books are *The Pelican History of the Church; Early Christian Thought and the Classical Tradition; Origen Contra Celsum; Alexandrian Christianity;* and *St. Ambrose on the Sacraments.*

JAMES E. GRIFFISS, a priest of the Episcopal Church, is William Adams Professor of Systematic Theology at Nashotah House, Wisconsin. Prior to his present appointment he was a Fellow and Tutor at the General Theological Seminary and Associate Professor of Theology at El Seminario Episcopal del Caribe in Puerto Rico. He is the author of *A Silent Path to God* (1980) and *Church, Ministry and Unity: A Divine Commission* (1983), and he has contributed to several collections of theological essays.

RICHARD A. NORRIS, JR., is a priest of the Diocese of New York and Professor of Church History at The Union Theological Seminary. He has taught at The Philadelphia Divinity School and The General Theological Seminary and has represented the

Episcopal Church in several ecumenical consultations. He is a member of the Inter-Anglican Theological and Doctrinal Commission. A student of early church history and patristic theology, he is also the author of a variety of books and articles.

ARTHUR MICHAEL RAMSEY served as the one hundredth Archbishop of Canterbury from 1961 to 1974. He was Professor of Divinity in the University of Durham, Canon of Durham Cathedral, and later became Regius Professor of Divinity at the University of Cambridge. He became Bishop of Durham in 1952 and Archbishop of York in 1956. He is a noted scholar, lecturer, author, and ecumenist. Among his many books are *The Gospel and the Catholic Church; The Glory of God and the Transfiguration of Christ; The Resurrection of Christ; God, Christ, and the World;* and *Holy Spirit.*

ARTHUR A. VOGEL was ordained bishop in 1971 and has been Bishop of West Missouri since 1973. He received a doctorate in philosophy from Harvard University, and taught philosophy and theology in colleges and theological seminaries for twenty-one years. Bishop Vogel has had wide ecumenical involvement, including sometime Co-Chairman of the Anglican-Roman Catholic Consultation in the U.S.A. and membership on both the first and second International Anglican-Roman Catholic Commissions. He has written nine books, among them, *Is the Last Supper Finished?; Body Theology;* and *The Jesus Prayer for Today.* He has also contributed to a number of other books and professional journals.

LOUIS WEIL received his doctorate in theology at the Catholic Institute in Paris and has been Professor of Liturgies and Church Music at Nashotah House since 1971. Prior to that time, he was a missionary priest in Puerto Rico, and lectured extensively in Latin America. He is the author of *Sacraments and Liturgy: The Outward Signs,* a study of the liturgical mentality of the Oxford Movement from the perspective of the liturgical concerns of our own time.